THE ENCOUNTER SERIES

The Bible, Politics, and Democracy

Essays by
Edward Dobson
Kenneth A. Myers
Ronald J. Sider
James W. Skillen
Corwin Smidt and Lyman Kellstedt
and
The Story of an Encounter by
Michael Cromartie

Edited and with a Foreword by
Richard John Neuhaus

WILLIAM B. EERDMANS PUBLISHING COMPANY
GRAND RAPIDS, MICHIGAN

Published by Wm. B. Eerdmans Publishing Co.
in cooperation with
The Rockford Institute Center on Religion & Society

Copyright © 1987 by Wm. B. Eerdmans Publishing Co.
255 Jefferson Ave. S.E., Grand Rapids, Mich. 49503

Library of Congress Cataloging-in-Publication Data:

The Bible, politics, and democracy.

   (Encounters series ; 5)
    1. Christianity and democracy.
2. Christianity and democracy—United States.
3. United States—Church history—20th century.
I. Dobson, Ed.
II. Neuhaus, Richard John.
III. Series: Encounter series (Grand Rapids, Mich.) ; 5.

BR115.P7B55   1987   261.7'0973   87-20095

ISBN 0-8028-0205-2

Contents

Foreword

If only everyone was a Christian, or if only Christians were more truly Christian, then we would know how to order society aright. So it is frequently said. Of course it isn't true.

The people gathered in the Billy Graham Center at Wheaton College for this conference were all Christians and, I have no doubt whatsoever, truly Christian. But, as becomes evident in the following pages, they are not agreed on the ordering of society. And even this is a select group. Had Christians of every variety been included, there certainly would not have been even the measure of agreement that this meeting manifested. The people at Wheaton agreed that—all in all, and taking alternatives into account—democracy is a good thing and Christians should support it.

The participants were all evangelicals, including evangelicals who call themselves fundamentalists. They begin from the premise that politicized evangelicalism has become a potent force in American public life and is likely to become more so. Since they agree that democracy is a good thing, their question is whether the evangelical insurgency is a good thing for democracy. The flow of conversation and concern is suggested by the title *The Bible, Politics, and Democracy*. The participants all had reason to be thinking about these questions for a long time. Much has been thought and much has been written about how Christians get from "Bible" to "politics." The third step is into territory less explored: How should biblical Christians who are politically engaged relate to democratic theory and practice?

Some participants suggested that Christian faith provides motivation and some truths that establish a metapolitical context but that there is no biblically prescribed right ordering of society. In the political realm, they say, we Christians operate by a prudential wisdom that is also available to non-Christians, the difference being that we are motivated by

vii

a desire to obey Christ in loving our neighbor. Others suggest there are some broad biblical mandates for the just structuring of society. But whether the judgment is based upon reason and regard for the neighbor or on an understanding of structural mandates, the consensus is that democracy is an appropriate form of governance in our kind of world.

As the reader might expect, participants had different ideas about what constitutes democracy. Democracy is not a disembodied concept but a historical and quite specific tradition of theory and practice. At issue here is "liberal democracy," a term that does not trip easily off the tongues of some evangelicals. It is liberal democracy as distinct from raw majoritarianism or the mob rule condemned by Aristotle and most thoughtful people. More particularly, it is the kind of liberal democracy that is preeminently—although all too imperfectly—represented by the democratic experiment that is the United States of America. These pages are an exploration of why Christians should give their assent, however qualified, to this kind of liberal democracy.

It was repeatedly said by participants at Wheaton that this kind of meeting is "unprecedented," and that may well be the case. A good deal of time was given to discussing the virtue of civility, since some participants felt that in the past they had not been treated civilly by other participants. In truth, during these days some people were meeting people against whom they had often polemicized but with whom they had never spoken. There was no agreement that civility is itself a religious virtue, but there was consent to the proposition that relations between people bound by the higher bond of Christian faith should be marked at least by civility. Although not all the participants would think of themselves as ecumenical, the encounter was surely an exercise in ecumenism. Indeed, it was ecumenism at its best: differences were not fudged but engaged, everyone came away from the encounter having learned, and the encounter itself advanced "the state of the question" under discussion.

I am grateful to all the participants, and most particularly to the presenters. Michael Cromartie did a first-class job of conveying the sense of the meeting through his "Story of an Encounter" in this volume. My thanks to colleagues in the Rockford Institute, John Howard, Allan Carlson, and Peter Berger. Paul Stallsworth, as always, put together the organizational pieces with good cheer and high competence, generously assisted by Joel Carpenter of the Billy Graham Center. And Davida Goldman, secretary of the Center on Religion and Society, puts us further in her debt by helping this manuscript to press.

THE ROCKFORD INSTITUTE   Richard John Neuhaus, Director
CENTER ON RELIGION AND SOCIETY
NEW YORK CITY

The Bible, Politics, and Democracy

Edward Dobson

When I was invited to write this essay, I was enthused at the prospect. However, the more involved I became in the project, the more I realized the difficulty of my task. The limitations of time and space prohibit an exhaustive study of the relationship between the Bible, politics, and democracy. Consequently, I have placed certain limits on the nature and purpose of my work.

First, this is not a political treatise. I have refrained from a technical discussion and definition of both "politics" and "democracy." I recognize the importance of such an endeavor, but I don't believe this essay to be the proper context in which to pursue it.

Second, this is not primarily a theological document. I have refrained from both theological debate and the fundamentalist bent toward "proof texts." I have avoided discussion of dispensationalism, covenantalism, and millenarianism. I have utilized Scripture where it is is necessary for the argument, however, even though I recognize that there will be differences of interpretation.

Third, I am cognizant that this essay is an *ex post facto* analysis. Fundamentalist political involvement is predicated on the motto "Ready, Fire, Aim." As such, we have influenced the political system at times with little cogitation or planning. In this paper I will attempt to move beyond our activity and determine the biblical presuppositions that initiated such action.

Fourth, I make no attempt to imply empirical objectivity. I acknowledge my bias. I am a fundamentalist and unashamed of it. I am defensive of Jerry Falwell and his politicized fundamentalism. I write

1

here not as an uninvolved critic but rather from within the heart of the movement.

Fifth, I make no attempt to analyze alternate biblical paradigms for social and political involvement. I will neither quote, refute, nor comment on Neuhaus or Niebuhr or anyone else. While the writings of others have merit in our current study, I have chosen not to respond to them. I am aware that by ignoring the previous research on this subject I am violating a generally accepted scientific rule for valid and reliable research. I have chosen to do so because fundamentalism is generally indifferent to the ideas of the intelligentsia and consequently little influenced by them.

Having discussed some of the factors that will govern my development of the subject, let me state what I will attempt to do. Based upon my involvement with fundamentalism and my perceptions of its political-social conscience, I will attempt to build a historical-biblical apologetic for its current belief and practice. In the first part of the essay I describe the catalysts that propelled fundamentalism into the political arena; in the second part, I examine the biblical presuppositions that govern such action; and in the last part I discuss the biblical perspective on democracy and reflect on our current participation. At times I discuss the tenets of the movement and at other times my own opinions. I suspect that in some instances the reader will find it difficult to draw a line between the two, for that is sometimes the case for me as well. In any event, I welcome the scrutiny of public debate and fully confess my own fallibility.

A HISTORICAL OVERVIEW

It was during the 1980 election that the fundamentalist movement marched into the mainstream of the political process. During that year, *Newsweek* stated, "What is clear on both the philosophical level—and in the rough-and-tumble arena of politics—is that the Falwells of the nation and their increasingly militant and devoted flock are a phenomenon that can no longer be dismissed or ignored."[1] This is the same movement that rejected the civil rights movement of the sixties and seventies and dismissed the evangelical call for social involvement in the fifties as irrelevant. Fundamentalism, which had rejected social and political involvement, was now pitching its tent in the public square. What precipitated the change?

In attempting to answer this question, it would ease the conscience to suggest that a new understanding of biblical truth was the catalyst.

---

1. "A Tide of Born-Again Politics," *Newsweek*, 15 September 1980, p. 36.

However, that was not the whole case. While we were certainly influenced by our commitment to Scripture, it was more the pressure of external forces that moved fundamentalism into its new posture of social and political concern. The early fundamentalist movement forged a loose-knit coalition against the threat of theological liberalism at the turn of the century. The new politicized fundamentalism, in like fashion, has forged a coalition of concerned Christians who feel threatened by the forces of secularism in the culture at large. The *Roe vs. Wade* decision of the Supreme Court which legalized abortion, the perceived removal of God from the public schools (I recognize that this is not a denial of his omnipresence), the breakdown of the traditional family, the pornography epidemic, the gay rights movement, the Equal Rights Amendment, the encroachment of the federal government on church affairs, and many other national and local issues generated a perception among fundamentalists that a new religion of secularism was evolving and that it threatened the extinction of the Judeo-Christian values. While we may debate the definitions of *secularism* and *humanism*, and while we may debate the seriousness of the threat they pose, the threat has nonetheless been perceived to be real. It was that perception more than anything else that forced fundamentalists to do something without first devising a theological justification.

One specific reaction to the increasing secularization of American society was the founding of the Moral Majority in 1979. With the assistance of James Kennedy, Charles Stanley, Tim LaHaye, and Greg Dixon, Jerry Falwell established this new nonpartisan political organization to promote morality in public life. The unique dimension of Moral Majority is that it is *not* a religious organization. It includes Jews, Protestants, Mormons, Catholics, nonreligious people—anyone who shares similar moral convictions. The underlying ideology was that which was advocated by the late Francis Schaeffer: co-belligerency. It involved bringing together people who shared similar convictions on a particular issue. Although Schaeffer was not directly associated with the Moral Majority, he certainly had tangential influence over it as an intellectual guru to both the organization and the increasingly militant fundamentalist movement in general.

However, this new strategy of cooperation with anyone who shared a common moral concern had been advocated by Carl F. H. Henry as early as 1947:

> Apart from denominational problems, it remains true that the evangelical, in the very proportion that the culture in which he lives is not actually Christian, must unite with non-evangelicals for social betterment if it is to be achieved at all, simply because the evangelical forces do not predominate. To say that evangelicalism

should not voice its convictions in a non-evangelical environment is simply to rob evangelicalism of its missionary vision.[2]

This newfound political cooperation was severely criticized by many. The political left branded it as manipulative power politics that smacked of McCarthyism. The religious right, such as Bob Jones, Jr., maligned Falwell for promoting religious ecumenicism. To the Joneses, Jerry Falwell became the "most dangerous man in America" because his conciliatory spirit went beyond that of Billy Graham. Falwell cooperated with Mormons, Jews, and Catholics; at least Graham went no further than mainline Protestant liberals. It is interesting to note that Henry predicted such criticism. "There are Fundamentalists who will insist immediately," he said, "that no evangelical has a right to unite with non-evangelicals in any reform."[3] It was evident, however, that the Moral Majority and politicized fundamentalism constituted a grassroots movement that would dramatically alter the balance of power in the current political process.

THE MORAL MAJORITY

In *The Fundamentalist Phenomenon*, Jerry Falwell outlines the basic moral position of the Moral Majority:

1. We believe in the separation of Church and State. Moral Majority, Inc., is a political organization providing a platform for religious and nonreligious Americans who share moral values to address their concerns in these areas. Members of Moral Majority, Inc., have no common theological premise. We are Americans who are proud to be conservative in our approach to moral, social, and political concerns.
2. We are pro-life. We believe that life begins at fertilization. We strongly oppose the massive "biological holocaust" that is resulting in the abortion of one and a half million babies each year in America. We believe that unborn babies have the right to life as much as babies that have been born. We are providing a voice and a defense for the human and civil rights of millions of unborn babies.
3. We are pro-traditional family. We believe that the only acceptable family form begins with a legal marriage of a man and woman. We feel that homosexual marriages and commonlaw marriages should not be accepted as traditional families. We oppose legislation that

2. Henry, *The Uneasy Conscience of Modern Fundamentalism* (Grand Rapids: Eerdmans, 1947), p. 80.
3. Henry, *Uneasy Conscience*, p. 79.

favors these kinds of "diverse family forms," thereby penalizing the traditional family. We do not oppose civil rights for homosexuals. We do oppose "special rights" for homosexuals who have chosen a perverted life-style rather than a traditional life-style.

4. We oppose the illegal drug traffic in America. The youth in America are presently in the midst of a drug epidemic. Through education, legislation, and other means we want to do our part to save our young people from death on the installment plan through illegal drug addiction.

5. We oppose pornography. While we do not advocate censorship, we do believe that education and legislation can help stem the tide of pornography and obscenity that is poisoning the American spirit today. Economic boycotts are a proper way in America's free-enterprise system to help persuade the media to move back to a sensible and reasonable moral stand. We most certainly believe in the First Amendment for everyone. We are not willing to sit back, however, while many television programs create cesspools of obscenity and vulgarity in our nation's living rooms.

6. We support the state of Israel and Jewish people everywhere. It is impossible to separate the state of Israel from the Jewish family internationally. Many Moral Majority members, because of their theological convictions, are committed to the Jewish people. Others stand upon the human and civil rights of all persons as a premise for support of the state of Israel. Support of Israel is one of the essential commitments of Moral Majority. No anti-Semitic influence is allowed in Moral Majority, Inc.

7. We believe that a strong national defense is the best deterrent to war. We believe that liberty is the basic moral issue of all moral issues. The only way America can remain free is to remain strong. Therefore we support the efforts of our present administration to regain our position of military preparedness—with a sincere hope that we will never need to use any of our weapons against any people anywhere.

8. We support equal rights for women. We agree with President Reagan's commitment to help every governor and every state legislature to move quickly to ensure that during the 1980s every American woman will earn as much money and enjoy the same opportunities for advancement as her male counterpart in the same vocation.

9. We believe ERA is the wrong vehicle to obtain equal rights for women. We feel that the ambiguous and simplistic language of the Amendment could lead to court interpretations that might put women in combat, sanction homosexual marriages, and financially penalize widows and deserted wives.

10. We encourage our Moral Majority state organizations to be autonomous and indigenous. Moral Majority state organizations may, from time to time, hold positions that are not held by the Moral Majority, Inc. national organization.

Falwell goes on to state what Moral Majority is not.

1. We are not a political party. We are committed to work within the multiple-party system in this nation. We are not a political party and do not intend to become one.
2. We do not endorse political candidates. Moral Majority informs American citizens regarding the vital moral issues facing our nation. We have no "hit lists." While we fully support the constitutional rights of any special-interest group to target candidates with whom they disagree, Moral Majority, Inc., has chosen not to take this course. We are committed to principles and issues, not candidates and parties.
3. We are not attempting to elect "born-again" candidates. We are committed to pluralism. The membership of Moral Majority, Inc., is so totally pluralistic that the acceptability of any candidate could never be based upon one's religious affiliation. Our support of candidates is based upon two criteria: (a) the commitment of the candidate to the principles that we espouse; (b) the competency of the candidate to fill that office.
4. Moral Majority, Inc., is not a religious organization attempting to control the government. Moral Majority is a special-interest group of millions of Americans who share the same moral values. We simply desire to influence government—not control government. This, of course, is the right of every American, and Moral Majority, Inc., would vigorously oppose any Ayatollah type of persons rising to power in this country.
5. We are not a censorship organization. We believe in freedom of speech, freedom of the press, and freedom of religion. Therefore while we do not agree that the Equal Rights Amendment would ultimately benefit the cause of women in America, we do agree with the right of its supporters to boycott those states that have not ratified the Amendment. Likewise, we feel that all Americans have the right to refuse to purchase products from manufacturers whose advertising dollars support publications and television programming that violate their own moral code.
6. Moral Majority, Inc., is not an organization committed to depriving homosexuals of their civil rights as Americans. While we believe that homosexuality is a moral perversion, we are committed to guaranteeing the civil rights of homosexuals. We do oppose the

efforts of homosexuals to obtain special privileges as a bona fide minority. And we oppose any efforts by homosexuals to flaunt their perversion as an acceptable life-style. We view heterosexual promiscuity with the same distaste which we express toward homosexuality.

7. We do not believe that individuals or organizations that disagree with Moral Majority, Inc., belong to an immoral minority. However, we do feel that our position represents a consensus of the majority of Americans. This belief in no way reflects on the morality of those who disagree with us or who are not involved in our organizational structures. We are committed to the total freedom of all Americans regardless of race, creed, or color.

Falwell concludes his section in *The Fundamentalist Phenomenon* by explaining how the Moral Majority hopes to achieve its goals:

1. By educating millions of Americans concerning the vital moral issues of our day. This is accomplished through such avenues as our newspaper, called the *Moral Majority Report*, a radio commentary by the same name, seminars, and other training programs conducted daily throughout the nation.
2. By mobilizing millions of previously "inactive" Americans. We have registered millions of voters and reactivated more millions of frustrated citizens into a special-interest group who are effectively making themselves heard in the halls of Congress, in the White House, and in every state legislature.
3. By lobbying intensively in Congress to defeat any legislation that would further erode our constitutionally guaranteed freedom and by introducing and/or supporting legislation that promotes traditional family and moral values, followed by the passage of a Human Life Amendment, which is a top priority of the Moral Majority agenda. We support the return of voluntary prayer to public schools while opposing mandated or written prayers. We are concerned to promote acceptance and adoption of legislation that keeps America morally balanced.
4. By informing all Americans about the voting records of their representatives so that every American, with full information available, can vote intelligently following his or her own convictions. We are nonpartisan. We are not committed to politicians or political parties; we are committed to principles and issues that we believe are essential to America's survival at this crucial hour. It is our desire to represent these concerns to the American public and allow it to make its own decisions on these matters.
5. By organizing and training millions of Americans who can become

moral activists. This heretofore silent majority in America can then help develop a responsive government which is truly "of the people, for the people" instead of "in spite of the people," which we have had for too many years now.

6. By encouraging and promoting non-public schools in their attempt to excel in academics while simultaneously teaching traditional family and moral values. There are thousands of non-public schools in America that accept no tax moneys. Some of these schools are Catholic, Fundamentalist, Jewish, Adventist, or of other faiths. Some are not religious. But Moral Majority, Inc., supports the right of these schools to teach young people not only how to make a living, but how to live.[4]

I apologize for quoting so extensively regarding the programs and practices of the Moral Majority, but I wanted to represent their style and substance carefully.

THE MANDATE FOR SOCIAL INVOLVEMENT

While it is relatively easy to discuss the current political positions of fundamentalism and the expression of those positions through the Moral Majority, it is infinitely more difficult to identify and define the theological presuppositions that support these political positions. At this point, a word of caution is in order. The combination of theological belief and political influence is dangerous. It can lead to an unrestrained use of power that violates our theological commitments and contradicts the pluralism of the American democratic experiment. As Richard J. Foster has pointed out, "When we are convinced that what we are doing is identical with the kingdom of God, anyone who opposes us *must* be wrong. . . . But when this mentality possesses us, we are taking the power of God and using it to our own needs."[5] Given this warning, what biblical directives give us the Christian mandate for social and political involvement? To answer this question, let me first discuss the general teaching of Scripture and then turn to some specific and often quoted passages.

For years many fundamentalists subscribed to a dichotomous worldview that magnified the sacred and minimized the secular. Political and social involvement were categorized as secular pursuits and hence

---

4. Falwell, *The Fundamentalist Phenomenon* (Garden City, N.Y.: Doubleday, 1980), pp. 189-92.

5. Foster, *Money, Sex and Power* (San Francisco: Harper & Row, 1985), pp. 178-79.

deemed secondary to spiritual pursuits, such as world evangelization. In fact, some fundamentalists, citing 2 Timothy 2:3-4, maintained that Christians should abstain from all such secular activity. This pietistic worldview is contradictory to the overall teaching of Scripture. As Christians, we recognize the lordship of Christ in every area of life—including the social and political arena. In both the Old and New Testaments there is a direct relationship between the proclamation of God's redemptive purpose and social concern. The Bible promises individual and national blessing for those who conform to God's law. The Bible warns of judgment for individuals and nations who violate God's law. The Bible calls for justice predicated upon God's righteousness. The Bible calls us to care for the poor, deliver the oppressed, and defend the defenseless. The message of the Old Testament prophets has clear social implications as does the message of John the Baptist. In fact, it was John's preaching against the incestuous marriage of Herod that precipitated his imprisonment and martyrdom. The healing ministry of Christ is a clear example of social involvement. The early church recognized the equality of all its members before God (1 Cor. 12:13). This teaching was in definite contrast to the social structure of that society. It is evident that the *evangel* cannot be isolated from social concern and involvement. Fundamentalists generally appeal to two major passages of Scripture to defend their political and social involvement.

1. The Great Commission

> And Jesus came and spake unto them saying, All power is given unto me in heaven and in earth. Go ye therefore, and teach all nations, baptizing them in the name of the Father, and of the Son, and of the Holy Ghost: Teaching them to observe all things whatsoever I have commanded you: and, lo, I am with you alway, even unto the end of the world. Amen.
>
> MATTHEW 28:18-20, KJV

Our consuming commitment to the Great Commission has been the major factor in the phenomenal growth of the fundamentalist movement. Realizing that the hope of humanity is not in social reform but rather in personal redemption, we have devoted our energies to building churches and establishing worldwide missionary movements. Evangelism has been and will continue to be our first priority. We believe that man is depraved and that personal faith in the redemptive work of Christ is the only means of salvation.

There are, however, some important social implications inherent in the Great Commission. First, Christ stated that *all* authority was given to him. We therefore believe in the sovereignty of God in political and social structures. The apostle Paul confirms this idea when he says, "Everyone must submit himself to the governing authorities, for there is no authority except that which God has established. The authorities that exist have been established by God" (Rom. 13:1, NIV). The Christian must also recognize that while we are obligated to political authority, our ultimate allegiance is to the authority of God and Scripture. Consequently, when human authority violates the clear authority of God, our obligation is to obey God and suffer the consequences of disobeying the human authority (Acts 4:19).

Second, the Great Commission calls us to "make disciples of all nations." This statement could be translated "disciple all nations." Read in the light of Christ's statement on authority, the Great Commission presents a call to bring all nations under the authority of Christ. The strategy for accomplishing this is to saturate the culture with biblical teaching. The responsibility of bringing the teaching of Christ to bear upon the nations is evident.

2. Light and Salt

> Ye are the salt of the earth: but if the salt have lost his savour, wherewith shall it be salted? it is thenceforth good for nothing, but to be cast out, and to be trodden under foot of men. Ye are the light of the world. A city that is set on an hill cannot be hid. Neither do men light a candle, and put it under a bushel, but on a candlestick; and it giveth light unto all that are in the house. Let your light so shine before men, that they may see your good works, and glorify your Father which is in heaven.
>
> MATTHEW 5:13-16, KJV

Christ reminded the disciples of their twofold obligation: they were to be salt and light. The illustration of salt implies both the concept of a covenant people and a moral conscience in the culture at large. In the Old Testament salt was symbolic of a covenant (Num. 18:19). In ancient Greek and Arab societies, legal agreements were confirmed by eating bread dipped in salt. Jesus is suggesting that we who are his disciples are the salt of the earth—we are his covenant people. Salt was also utilized in ancient cultures for preserving and flavoring meat. Jesus seems to be implying that we are also a moral preservative and ethical conscience to the society in which we live. As representatives of his righteous standards, we should be involved in preserving Judeo-Christian values as foundational for the health of the society in which we live.

Jesus also refers to us as the light of the world. Most commentators interpret this to mean that we have an evangelistic obligation to society. We are to shed the light of the gospel on the dark world around us. While this is certainly true, Jesus is also speaking of the light of our "good deeds" (v. 16). We are to be a moral conscience (salt), but at the same time we are to demonstrate that moral standard through our good deeds (light). In other words, we have no right to call for justice unless we are ourselves just in dealing with others. For example, we have no right to call for legislative changes to eliminate abortion on demand (salt) if we are unwilling to care for those thousands of new babies whose lives will be saved because of the new legislation (light).

THE DOCTRINE OF DEMOCRACY?

Having established a historical and biblical perspective on the Bible and politics, let me now turn to the issue of democracy. More specifically, we must address the question of what the Bible has to say about the democratic ideas expressed in the American experience. In answering this question, a number of options are available. First, one might argue that America is a "chosen nation" and as such its form of government is inspired by God. This viewpoint, which was advocated by Peter Marshall and David Manuel in *The Light and the Glory*, defends the proposition that America was founded as a Christian nation and that it must return to its roots. As fundamentalists, we believe that God was sovereignly involved in the founding of this nation but that he was no more sovereignly involved in its affairs than he is in the affairs of any other nation. While we have called for the "Christianizing" of America, we have not thereby been calling for a return to the elevation of Christianity to the minimization or exclusion of other religions or nonreligious ideologies. Our choice of terminology was unfortunate, and we have since apologized. We were calling for a return to moral values as expressed in the Judeo-Christian ethic.

A second option in addressing the relationship of the Bible to democracy would be to establish a theology of democracy. Jerry Combee and Cline Hall identify what they call the "doctrines of democracy" as follows:

> Equality of rights . . .
> Liberty for all . . .
> Limited government . . .
> Government by consent of the governed . . .
> The right of revolution . . .[6]

---

6. Combee and Hall, *Designed for Destiny* (Wheaton, Ill.: Tyndale, 1985), p. 47.

While there is certainly merit in these ideas, I find it difficult to accept them as doctrines that establish democracy as the exclusive standard for political structures. I find two major objections to such a position. First, it seems to me that there are also biblical ideas that would substantiate socialism as an acceptable expression of biblical truth in a political structure. In fact, when I was a college student, I encountered serious difficulties when I spoke to five hundred missions students on the merits of socialism. The second objection is that the truly biblical political system is a theocracy, God ruling over the cosmos. Nearly all fundamentalists believe that Christ will come to this earth and establish his kingdom for one thousand years. Our ultimate hope is not in the transitory political systems of this present age but in the prospect of the second coming of Jesus Christ. He will establish justice, righteousness, and peace upon the earth. It seems to me that while other political options may be close to biblical truth, they certainly constitute a distant second to a theocracy.

A third option in addressing the relationship of the Bible to democracy would be to establish moral (biblical) principles that transcend political structures. If these ideals can be articulated, then the question would be which political system best incorporates these doctrines. It is this particular line of thinking I would like to pursue. In fact, I would suggest three overarching biblical truths that should guide our thinking in regard to political systems.

1. The Principle of Life

> *And the LORD God formed man of the dust of the ground, and breathed into his nostrils the breath of life; and man became a living soul.*
>
> GENESIS 2:7, KJV

Life is a gift from God. As Christians we must recognize that only God Almighty can create life and that we have an obligation to honor and protect it. There are several propositions that emerge from this principle of life.

We must protect the existence of a human life. Since life is a gift from God and since we believe that life begins at conception, we believe that abortion is the murder of human life and as such we are committed to promote legislative and judicial relief from this genocide. Our concern for human life goes beyond abortion to euthanasia and infanticide. In their book, *Whatever Happened to the Human Race?* Francis A. Schaeffer and Dr. C. Everett Koop ask, "Will a society which has assumed the right to kill infants in the womb—because they are unwanted, imperfect, or merely inconvenient—have difficulty in assuming the right

to kill other human beings, especially older adults who are judged unwanted, deemed imperfect physically or mentally, or considered a possible social nuisance?"[7]

We must promote the dignity of human life. We believe that we are
created in the image of God and as such we have great worth and merit.
Consequently, we must do all that we can to enhance a person's dignity.
We are opposed to any economic system that robs people of their worth
and denies them their God-given creativity. We are concerned about the
poor, the oppressed, and the disenfranchised. We reject Marxism as an
equal-opportunity oppressor, we reject socialism as mutually shared poverty, and we reject welfarism as mutually shared hopelessness. While we
must care for those who cannot help themselves, we must promote a
system that restores dignity and worth to each individual. To rob people
of this opportunity is to deny them part of God's creative intent.

We must promote the equality of human life. "Red and yellow,
black and white, all are precious in his sight." These are more than the
words of a simple Sunday school song. They are the expression of an
important biblical truth. Fundamentalists do not believe in the universal
fatherhood of God or the universal brotherhood of man. However, we do
accept the fact that we are all equal before God. The New Testament
clearly prohibits prejudicial and racist attitudes and actions (James 2).
Such behavior is antithetical to Christianity. Fundamentalists should
have been at the forefront of the civil rights movement. We were wrong
and we do not intend to sit by and suggest by silence that we sanction any
system that denies people their equality before God and each other.

The Principle of Freedom

> *And the LORD God commanded the man, saying, Of every tree of
> the garden thou mayest freely eat: But of the tree of the knowledge of
> good and evil, thou shalt not eat of it: for in the day that thou eatest
> thereof thou shalt surely die.*
>
> GENESIS 2:16-17, KJV

Man was created *posse peccare et posse non peccare.* He was created with
the freedom to choose. As fundamentalists, we are opposed to any system
of government that seeks to oppress its constituents by eliminating their
freedom of choice. We are committed to protecting the rights of human
beings to choose their work and worship, their homes and cars, their
vacations and recreation, their friends and colleagues, their groups and

---

7. Schaeffer and Koop, *Whatever Happened to the Human Race?* (Old
Tappan, N.J.: Fleming H. Revell, 1979), p. 89.

associations. We believe that we must be free to express our opinions and oppose others with whom we disagree. We believe that the most important choice is the freedom to worship God according to the dictates of our conscience. This religious freedom incorporates not only the freedom to worship but the freedom to preach, to teach, to evangelize, and to exercise our responsibility to address the social and moral problems of society. We believe that this basic human right of freedom of choice transcends the dictates of the state and is rooted in our dignity as human beings created in the image of God.

3. The Principle of Sin

And God saw that the wickedness of man was great in the earth, and that every imagination of the thoughts of his heart was only evil continually.

GENESIS 6:5, KJV

Wherefore, as by one man sin entered into the world, and death by sin; and so death passed upon all men, for that all have sinned.

ROMANS 5:12, KJV

Fundamentalists believe in the depravity of human nature. Louis Berkhof, in commenting on the total depravity of man, states that "The contagion of his sin at once spread through the entire man, leaving no part of his nature untouched, but vitiating every power and faculty of body and soul."[8] We believe that human beings are fallen creatures living in a fallen world. This theological doctrine has an important bearing on our understanding of biblical truth and its relevance for political and social involvement. First, in light of man's depravity, we believe that his ultimate hope is not in the reformation of society but rather in personal salvation through the gospel of Jesus Christ. While social and political concern is legitimate, it can never replace the priority of calling fallen mankind to repentance and faith in Jesus Christ. In this sense, the church must always remain the church. Second, man's depravity has clear implications for political governance. Man's inherent quest for power and domination, his propensity for evil and destruction, demand a system of governance that is predicated upon higher laws and limited government that respects the rights and freedoms of all. For this reason we believe that the future of the American democratic society is predicated upon our allegiance and adherence to the principles of the

---

8. Berkhof, *Systematic Theology*, rev. ed. (Grand Rapids: Eerdmans, 1949), pp. 225-26.

Judeo-Christian ethic. Consequently, we are opposed to the current secularization of our society and believe that the exorcism of religion from the public square will inevitably result in the elimination of an objective higher moral standard. We will in essence lose the substantive foundation for the moral and ethical standards that guarantee the freedoms we now enjoy.

We have been discussing the moral principles that transcend political structures: the principle of life, the principle of freedom, and the principle of sin. While it is relatively easy to define and discuss these principles, it is infinitely more complicated to apply them to the complex problems of the twentieth century. In fact, these principles could be brought into conflict in solving the social evils of society. The sin of apartheid in South Africa is such an example. First, apartheid is clearly a violation of the principle of life. It denies the dignity and equality of human beings under God. Christians ought to oppose it and bring whatever pressure necessary to eliminate it. However, when one calls for disinvestment and a further destabilization of the economy, the principle of freedom enters into the formula. South Africa is threatened by a Marxist-Leninist takeover. If such were to happen, the basic human right of freedom would be eliminated in favor of a godless Marxist state. Consequently, there are Christians calling for disinvestment in the name of equality and Christians opposing disinvestment in the name of freedom. Both positions have merit. The issue then becomes one of hierarchical moral principles. It becomes a matter of choosing the overriding moral principle for a complex moral problem.

The issue of nuclear armament is also an issue of competing moral principles. Our commitment to the protection of human life has important implications for nuclear arms. The possibility of nuclear annihilation is a threat to the human race. As such, it is legitimate for Christians to oppose nuclear arms. However, our belief in the depravity of man forces us to take the threat of Soviet expansionism seriously. Communist regimes have murdered more than 140 million people since 1917 and denied human rights to millions more. Consequently, opposing Communism is an act that protects basic human rights. In order to protect the freedom of the Western world, it is necessary to build an armament that will prevent the Soviets from further world domination. Therefore, the principles of life, freedom, and depravity are brought into conflict.

We have discussed three moral imperatives. The question now becomes which political structure is most suited to the expression and protection of these values. I would suggest that the answer to this question is a democratic political system. This is not a theological answer predicated on a series of proof texts but a pragmatic answer rooted in historical evidence. Democratic governance guarantees the equality and dignity of human life. Democratic governance protects our basic human rights and guarantees our freedom of religion. It allows us to be what God has called us to be and to do what God has called us to do. Democratic governance is a governance of limited power and a system of checks and balances. It inhibits man's quest for absolute power and domination. While other political systems offer some of these benefits, democracy offers all of them. For Christians, it promises the best alternative for the expression of our values in a fallen world.

FUNDAMENTALIST METHODOLOGY

In order to understand politicized fundamentalism, one must understand what we believe and how we express that belief to the culture at large. In the March 1985 issue of the *Fundamentalist Journal* (pp. 14-15) I wrote an editorial dealing with this issue of private religion and public morality. The following is a short excerpt from that editorial.

1. *Private religion: what we believe.* Our faith is deeply rooted in our commitment to the inspired and inerrant Word of God—the Bible. We believe that the Scriptures are without error not only in matters of religion but also in matters of history, science, and the cosmos. As such they are the authoritative guide for faith and practice. We believe that Jesus Christ is the virgin-born Son of God, the promised Messiah of Old Testament Scripture. We believe he died a substitutionary and vicarious death on the cross and was literally and bodily raised from the dead three days later. We believe that faith in Christ is the only way to heaven and that we are commanded to preach the gospel around the world. We believe that Jesus Christ is coming back to this planet to establish his kingdom and to reign.

In this theological domain of our private religion, we seek no change, conciliation, or compromise. When we state that our objective is to evangelize the world, we mean exactly that. We fully recognize the political and social implications of such a statement. When we state that salvation is predicated upon faith in Christ and not baptism, confession, or church membership, we mean exactly that. These statements are not anti-Catholic, anti-Jewish, or anti-Muslim; they are expressions of what we believe. We have always believed and preached the same message, and we do not intend to change for the sake of being accepted according to the standards of others.

The point of tension seems to lie more with our methods than with our message. Sometimes we exercise our religious objectives in a way that destroys the impact of our message. Paul admonishes us to "speak the truth in love" (Eph. 4:15). Our message must be tempered with a love that accepts others—even those with whom we strongly disagree. Extremists who declare that the papacy is of the Anti-Christ or who dehumanize others with emotional declarations of their own bigotry are insensitive and lack the love of Christ.

2. *Public morality: what we practice.* As fundamentalists we believe that the First Amendment prohibits the establishment of a state religion and thereby protects the rights of all religions. At the same time, it does not advocate the exorcism of God and religion from society. We believe that religion must neither dominate the political process nor be dominated by it. We must be free to worship God according to the dictates of our conscience, and we must be free to exercise our political rights as good citizens. But in exercising our political responsibilities, we have been misunderstood by some, and a little clarification is in order.

First, we are not seeking to make America a Christian nation. We are concerned about the erosion of the basic values expressed in the Judeo-Christian tradition, and we believe we must protect those values within our society.

Second, we are committed to an America that is pluralistic in the broadest sense. We desire to protect the rights of all minorities—whether or not they share our faith. For example, we disagree with the doctrine of the Mormon church, but we must protect the Mormons' right to have their missionaries knock on our doors, so we can have the liberty to knock on their doors.

Third, we are committed to principles, not political parties. We are committed to protecting the life of the unborn and defending the nation of Israel. We are concerned about the growing industries of pornography and illegal drugs and the increasing intrusion of government into religious affairs. We are proponents of a strong defense as the best deterrent to nuclear war, and from that position of strength negotiate the verifiable elimination of nuclear weapons. When political platforms converge with our agenda we support them, and when they do not we oppose them. We advocate co-belligerency with others who share our moral, social, and political concerns. We are exercising our American citizenship and doing what the National Council of Churches, the National Association for the Advancement of Colored People, the National Education Association, and other special interest and minority groups have been doing for years. When others suggest that we should be silent, we wonder if their only concern is that we threaten their position in the political process.

Fourth, we seek to influence the political process in the highest tradition of American politics. We reject the use of manipulative power politics and inhumane methods to accomplish our goals. While we may battle with others in the process, we must live with them in peace as fellow Americans. We must practice the "Golden Rule" in all our relationships.

Biblical Obedience and Political Thought: Some Reflections on Theological Method

Kenneth A. Myers

The question posed to this gathering asks about biblical obedience and political thought, which I assume is the question of how we obey Scripture as we think about politics. My first reaction is to ring changes on the question and suggest that our task also has to do with biblical thought and political obedience—that is, how (not what) we think about the Bible as we attempt to be obedient to God in the political realm. If we believe that it is God's will that we somehow work to change the world, we must certainly both understand the Word and the world and understand *how* we understand them.

Knowing our host, I assume that the emphasis on obedient thinking was not accidental. Time-consuming reflection on the nature of our reflection may seem to some so much intellectual fiddling while Rome burns. But since the cause of discord among Christians concerned about this world is in large measure a matter of differences about methods of analysis—differences that will not be self-correcting—such reflection is time well spent.

My approach to the question at hand will reflect my own vocation as a journalist, and I will raise more questions about the subject than I will offer answers. I have not been trained as a political philosopher or historian and have minimal theological training. I proceed from the perspective of an interested observer—interested in political questions and interested in trying to decipher how evangelicals respond to them. Of late, I have been interested in observing such responses and comparing them to the responses of other communities of thought.

The question that has haunted me for the past few years is why

19

some evangelicals seem to be eager to bear a sputtering torch, to become the eager champions of programs and perspectives on American political and social life that have, in the larger community addressing questions of public policy, come to seem either foolish or at least open to serious debate. Specifically, I have been disheartened to see a replica of the mentality of the sixties emerge in nominally evangelical circles. Such a mentality expresses to one degree or another the belief that America is the chief cause of suffering and evil in the world, that Western culture has no redeeming or redeemable values, and that the malignancies of Marxist-Leninist regimes are purely a natural reaction to American bellicosity.

It is most fascinating that such a version of the world should re-emerge at precisely the time when many of those who not long ago believed such things and preached revolution on behalf of their beliefs are now repudiating them and adopting a stance much more consistent with the liberal tradition in America. That tradition has been unapologetically prodemocratic and anticommunist and boasts a long list of respected adherents, many of them prominent intellectuals. Today, such a tradition is regaining credibility in such places as the pages of *The New Republic* and *The Partisan Review*. But, irony of ironies, the stance of historical American liberalism is regarded as reactionary and uninformed in many evangelical circles.

Why is it that among educated evangelicals there is so little appreciation for the rich intellectual heritage that explored, defined, and often defended the American experiment in democracy? Part of the answer is in the ignorance among evangelicals of that intellectual heritage. Anticommunism is associated with Carl MacIntyre rather than with Raymond Aron. Praising democracy is something for right-wing red-neck God-and-country good ol' boys, not for sophisticated religionists such as we.

Another part of the answer is certainly that a faith in democracy among the likes of, say, Sidney Hook or Karl Popper may have become a substitute for true religion. It need not have so become. It certainly was not for other champions of liberty such as Michael Polanyi or Jacques Maritain.

A large part of the answer is in a lack of reflection about how we might properly think about such things. As evangelicals we have almost no tradition of social ethics. There are those among us who are so eager to distance themselves from an apathetic or reactionary past that they avoid any premises or conclusions that sound remotely as if they will bless the status quo. And in that rush, little time has been taken to acknowledge the significant theological differences in our community—some of them fundamental differences. We have taken a patchwork systematic theological tradition and an even more threadbare set of hermeneutical suppositions and tried to reupholster a rapidly fraying political and social fabric with rhetoric about discipleship and the kingdom. Such efforts may make matters worse.

The methodological problems of evangelical thought about matters political seem to come from at least four general areas: (1) a neglect of the different functions of and relations among biblical exegesis, systematic theology, the development of theory, empirical analysis, and the formulation of policy; (2) a lack of sustained attention to the ramifications of various doctrines to political thought; (3) a tendency to make of political questions an exercise in getting the answers right in the abstract and thereby ignoring the real world; and (4) the temptation to succumb to popular but problematic theoretical frameworks for analysis, either out of ignorance or in the interest of winsomeness. Each of these shortcomings hampers biblical obedience in political thought. I shall address the first of these at length and touch on the other three.

EXEGESIS, THEOLOGY, THEORY, ANALYSIS, POLICY

Long before they ever heard of praxis-oriented theology, evangelicals pursued obedience with a practical attitude. As much as people complain about moribund orthodoxy among evangelicals, I have met few evangelicals who could produce an outline of orthodoxy but have known many with strong convictions about a long list of matters of practice. Among our communal ironies is the fact that the most durable tie that binds evangelicals is a belief in conversion, but we have never agreed on a theory that explains how or why one is converted or what it will subsequently affect. Now that concern about political and social affairs is almost unanimously recognized as something worthy of evangelical involvement, such sloppy habits of mind are an even greater moral hazard. Motivated but misinformed and intellectually careless people are raw meat to unscrupulous demagogues. Since politics is the arena of temporal power, an arena of life and death, evangelical zeal about political action must be informed by a wisdom for which I'm afraid our tradition has not well prepared us.

As we approach this arena trying to be wise, we must first acknowledge that while we as a community recognize the authority of Scripture, we have many conflicting views of what the Bible in fact teaches on many matters. Unfortunately, the adjective *biblical* is too easily accepted as meaning "true to God's Word," when it more often means only "derived from God's Word." One of the confusing paradoxes in the evangelical world is the common reluctance on the part of leaders to insist publicly that one's opponents, who are asserting a "biblical" position, are nonetheless (in one's opinion) wrong. So, for example, nuclear deterrence and nuclear pacifism are both put forth publicly as "biblical options" (although in private each side may say that theirs is the only *right* position).

Take for another example the curious sight of Christians who advocate the just-war position and Christians who are pacifist-isolationists trying to come to some meaningful agreement on, say, U.S. foreign policy in Latin America. How can they hope to agree at the level of policy when they don't agree on the ground rules, when they disagree on the teaching of the Scriptures on the basic questions of war and peace and the nature of the state? One side questions the validity of "national security interests" and rules out in principle the use of force under any circumstances. The other side regards the pacifist-isolationist stance as dangerous and ultimately immoral, representing a refusal to oppose in any effective way injustice and tyranny in the world and a sacrifice of the rights and lives of innocent people to unscrupulous powers. One side says the Sermon on the Mount applies univocally to international relations; the other side denies it. One side says that Christians are obliged to beat swords into plowshares now; the other side says that such activity is an effect of God's eschatological intervention into history not to be anticipated by the church. One side says that the Bible teaches that killing in war is murder; the other side says that killing in war is divinely warranted and even at times required of obedient Christians.

Both sides argue from the Scripture, but both sides can't be right. To assert that there are sincere Christians on both sides (and at many points in between) is sociologically interesting but useless from the standpoint of discovering the truth. Since our goal is not just to have derived our positions from Scripture but to be obedient to the intention of the Holy Spirit who inspired the text, we should feel uncomfortable implying that the Spirit is telling one group that killing in warfare is in keeping with Christian obedience and simultaneously telling another group that such killing is a sin.

Deciding to ignore those differences for strategic reasons may sometimes be appropriate. But prudently ignoring the distinctions is not the same as saying the distinctions don't matter at all. Unfortunately, we have come to the point where this logical leap has been made by a large portion (if not the majority) of evangelicals. Ignoring such differences will be an obstacle to our discussion of political issues.

One of the points we must settle (or at least acknowledge our differences regarding it) concerns the relationship between reason and revelation as it pertains to political thought. On a popular level, evangelicals have tended to see the debate about reason and revelation only as a question of authority. But it also involves a question of epistemology. Pertinent to the present discussion is the question of whether political philosophy is a matter principally informed by general revelation and reason or a matter principally informed by biblical exegesis.

Some may say that the doctrine of the sufficiency of Scripture requires that behavior in all areas of life be governed by biblical truth. Governed, yes, but not fully defined.

It is generally agreed that the Bible is not a textbook of any kind. It does not spell out fully formed theoretical outlines in any discipline, not even in theology. But acknowledging this, evangelicals still run the risk of asking too much of the Scriptures. Such a risk can be mitigated by careful attention to the separate phases of exegesis, the forming of systematic theology, and the development of theory. We begin by recognizing that a political philosophy cannot be deduced or inferred from the Scriptures. We have no good reason to suppose that the Bible will provide us with all the raw material we need for the framing of political philosophy, though it is obviously the source of necessary and authoritative premises that govern our thinking.

Instead of merely constructing a deductive argument, we move from particular texts of Scripture to our interpretation of those texts to our systematic understanding of the teaching of the Bible as a whole. Then, girded with this systematic understanding, we can move out beyond the limits of Scripture to develop theories in various disciplines by proceeding with a rational process of observation and reflection always governed by, checked by, and corrected by the conclusions or ramifications of the inspired Word, interpreted and understood systematically.

From the vantage point of a theologically informed theory, we then strive to understand the world. We observe historical and intellectual patterns, anomalies, and crises. We assess the merits and demerits of historical movements not only in light of their abstract orthodoxy but in light of what effects they have now and what they augur for future events. Finally, we can form some notion of possible policies, always attentive to the complexities and the limitations of our knowledge, always cognizant of the length of the path from the pure Word of God to our plans. And so while rooted in Scripture, governed by Scripture, we avoid proof-texting.

Such a process obviously involves the recognition of the role of empirical analysis in the process of argument. If the major premise of my argument is drawn from Scripture (e.g., God hates injustice), but the minor premise is based on empirical analysis (e.g., capitalism is unjust), I cannot assert that the conclusion (e.g., God hates capitalism) is simply the teaching of the Word of God. I *can* say that God hates injustice and that, in my judgment, capitalism is unjust. But the truth of the minor premise is not determined either by the truth of the major premise or by the validity of the argument. Continually repeating the major premise with prophetic fervor will not demonstrate the truth of the minor premise. Only sustained examination of the facts and argumentation from them can do that.

One of the worst types of proof-texting involves a failure to take the

progress of redemptive history into consideration. I am especially concerned about appeals to the Bible, both Old and New Testaments, for
normative models of the good state. Such appeals are most often made
with Old Testament texts in view. According to my own theological
tradition, the law of Israel and the indictments uttered by the prophets
were inextricable from the administration of the covenant. Israel was a
type of the eschatological kingdom of heaven. The closest modern ana-
logue to Israel is the church, not the United States or any contemporary
state. As we read the Old Testament, our first obligation is to understand
the text in its original historical setting and then find the analogies in our
own day. True, Israel is a nation and the United States is a nation, but
that is slender grounds for insisting on the normativeness of any given
application of any given text.

Israel had an obligation to be a convenantally righteous nation, to
meet standards that God did not establish for, say, Egypt. Israel was a
holy nation as no nation before or since could claim to be. Its national
identity was a mechanism of God's redemptive work in a unique way. In
every aspect of its national life as ordered by God, Israel was anticipating
the character of the people of God upon the consummation of redemptive history. Its obedience or disobedience in civil matters had
consequences more like the apostasy of a church than the tyranny of a
modern nation. The tyranny of Egypt was certainly an offense to God,
but it was not compounded by the breaking of the covenant. Egypt's
oppression of the poor was a civil sin of a state never in peculiar relation to
God. Israel's oppression of the poor was a civil sin *and* a mockery of God's
electing love and grace.

To regard either the law (as do my postmillennialist friends and
some of my premillennialist friends) or the prophets (as do many of my
premillennialist and amillennialist friends) as speaking univocally to the
United States begs too many questions, to say the least. There are certainly many principles for the development of political thinking within
the Old Testament. But any application of a text that ignores its original
context in redemptive history, especially the relationship of the covenant
to the original recipients of the text, must be regarded as of dubious value.

There is no a priori reason to believe that any given aspects of the
law of Israel are normative for the U.S. civil code. Each provision of the
law must be considered in turn, in an attempt to determine whether the
law is based in the nature of God itself or on permanent relations of men
in the present phase of redemptive history on the one hand, or whether
the law is based on a temporary or provisional relationship among men or
a positive command of God peculiar to a particular time and place on the
other hand. Unless we have established that the law is normative for our
age, we must not assume it to be. Similarly, we must not take the
declamations of the prophets out of their eschatological context and

regard them as timeless wisdom. The citation of 2 Chronicles 7:14 as an emblem of American moral renewal is unwarranted, if well-intentioned. The recitation of Isaiah's prophecy about beating swords into plowshares without attention to the crucial events in the text that must precede this eschatological pacifism is irresponsible.

I am not dismissing the Old Testament; I am merely trying to respect its intentions. The Old Testament revelation defines such matters as the nature of man, the effects of sin, and the scope of redemption. Such doctrines, formulated in conjunction with New Testament teaching, have many ramifications for our political thinking. Unfortunately, many of these doctrines are obscured in the attempt to reduplicate Israel's national polity or to anticipate the eschatological kingdom in ways we are not meant to. Until Christ returns, the church is God's new holy nation, and God has postponed his judgment. Our thinking about political obedience must keep this in view.

A final note on hermeneutics seems in order. In looking for personal guidance, evangelicals have often treated the Bible like Aesop's Fables, as a collection of moral tales with parallels for our own lives. A similar approach is evident in the way they apply it to social and political matters. As David did thus, so we should do thus. As the prophets condemned such and such, so we should condemn such and such. This is another way of ignoring redemptive history. Neither the exodus nor Joseph's experience in Egypt nor the hubris of Saul can be taken as normative paradigms for political reflection apart from considerations of the role of the event in the history of redemption and determinations of appropriate analogies in our own place in redemptive history.

The same principle holds true for applying the New Testament. We cannot assume that the communal life of the church depicted in Acts or Christ's refusal to assume temporal power are normative models for modern behavior for Christians. It is a standard (if rarely observed) hermeneutical practice to insist that historical narrative is not normative unless there is an indication that it is meant to be interpreted as such.

RAMIFICATIONS OF DOCTRINE

Many of the political ramifications of biblical teaching stem from the biblical doctrine of sin. This may be the single most significant theological heading for political thinking, since sin shapes the context for all of our political activity. Without sin, there would be no need for the power of the sword. Apart from a recognition of the effects of sin, the power of the sword becomes tyrannical.

The state does not exist to abolish sin. It does not exist to remake man, thereby undoing the effects of sin. It exists to restrain the effects of sin and to arbitrate among sinful peoples in the interest of civil justice. Eschatological justice is God's to exercise; the power of the sword is in a sense a type of final judgment reminding all that wrongdoing will be punished. But since all wrongdoing deserves death, and no state has ever practiced capital punishment for all offenses (including sins in the heart), it is obvious that the state does not have the calling of establishing eschatological justice. Civil justice must be understood as some minimum standard of equity and lawfulness rooted in general revelation rather than in special revelation. Sodom and Gomorrah were apparently held accountable by God to social standards available in general revelation, as were many other Old Testament figures and nations. Christians, having access to special revelation, must make appeals for civil justice to standards accessible to (if ruthlessly denied by) all sinful men and women.

The doctrine of sin also suggests that power will tend to be abused by sinful people and thus that power should not be concentrated in a few hands. Such wisdom is behind the establishment of the three branches of the U.S. government, as well as behind the notion of constitutional democracy more generally. When ecclesiastical, economic, educational, and other spheres are further separated from the exclusive hand of government, some of the potential tyrannies of sinful people are mitigated, though imperfectly.

It should be noted that Christians advancing the argument for the superiority of democratic government are not obligated to show that the Bible teaches democracy but merely that, in our sinful world and specifically at this time in history, democratic polity best secures the aims of civil justice, as well as advancing the cause of peace.[1]

Another aspect of the biblical doctrine of sin that must be mentioned is the locus of sin in the individual will. The notion of "sinful structures" seems to me a notion more referred to than clearly understood. Since it introduces a number of potentially insidious corollaries, it is essential that evangelicals who wish to use such language use it carefully and correctly. Lacking the time to discuss it fully, I raise two series of questions and make two references for further reflection.

Can the doctrine of "sinful structures" be formulated in such a way as to avoid the notion of collective guilt, a notion that is fundamental to

---

1. See Peter L. Berger, "Democracy for Everyone?" *Commentary*, September 1983, pp. 31-36; Richard John Neuhaus, *Christianity and Democracy* (Washington, 1981); and R. J. Rummel, "On Fostering a Just Peace," *International Journal on World Peace*, Autumn 1984, pp. 4-15. Rummel deals with the role of "peace-fostering" and contends on philosophical and empirical grounds that "spreading and enhancing the institutions of freedom fosters a global and just peace."

acts of terrorism and other violence? In other words, is it in fact biblically necessary that, for example, because I am a white American, I am personally guilty for all the evil done by white Americans as a class? If so, am I guilty for all evil they have done *qua* whites or *qua* Americans, or both? Am I guilty for all the evils done by black Americans, or by white Canadians? Does the biblical principle of solidarity require the notion that every evil perpetrated by any collective in which I can conceivably be included is justly attributed to me? If so, can I justly be punished for such evils? If a terrorist kills an American civilian at random because of alleged evils perpetrated by American military or political forces, is the terrorist not fulfilling the logic of the doctrine of structural evil as commonly put forth? Since the Bible teaches the solidarity of the human race (e.g., in teaching about the imputation of Adam's sin), is every person guilty for every other person's evil? Finally, how can the doctrine of the sinlessness of Christ be reconciled with such notions, given Christ's complicity with an evil regime generally by being a member of society and specifically by paying taxes?

The second matter about which I have questions is more practical. Why do I rarely hear any talk about *good* structures? In reading the works of the so-called radical Christians, I have yet to see references to good structures. I recognize that the understanding of Paul's reference to "principalities and powers" shared by H. Berkhof, John H. Yoder, and Jim Wallis suggests strongly that there are no such things as good structures, that all structures inherently tend toward evil. Is this the view of all those who emphasize structural evil?

Gerhart Niemeyer has reflected thoughtfully on the question of structures and evil in at least two articles: "Structures, Revolutions and Christianity" (*Center Journal*, Winter 1981, pp. 79-99) and "A 'Church' without a Name?" (*Center Journal*, Summer 1982, pp. 107-19).

What I have attempted to do in this section is spell out just a few of the ramifications of the doctrine of sin for political thought. Rather than spending all of our time rehearsing biblical teaching about the state, evangelicals should spend more time considering the consequences of other loci of theology for political philosophy.

TEMPTATION TO ABSTRACTION

The charge of "utopianism" has often been leveled at Christians engaged in political thought. Two varieties of utopianism are particularly tempting to evangelicals. One is the formulation of political philosophy apart from any consideration of the world as it exists. To develop a program for the pursuit of peace and justice without attention to the contemporary forces that disrupt peace and ignore justice is to develop a utopian vision, a vision for "no place." I am surprised at the conclusions of my friends whose language is peppered with such words as *praxis* and *contextualization* and yet whose thinking seems to have little historical or geopolitical tethering. The context of their praxis seems to be an ideological world picture that has little to do with this world.

It is never enough for us to concoct notions of perfect government. We must move beyond the ideal to developing strategies for biblical obedience in imperfect states, the world of wheat and tares, where unregenerate men and women will continue to wield power. This is why the recent emphasis on structures could be very healthful. The task for the Christian political thinker is to develop mechanisms that best secure civil justice for all, even when power is issued to people with no fear of divine justice.

If I am behaving charitably, I do not compare my wife with a theoretical perfect wife but with the feasible alternatives. I can recognize her shortcomings without feeling the obligation of pronouncing the full wrath of God upon her. She is a mixture of virtue and vice deserving both praise and exhortation. Perhaps in assessing American democracy as a political experiment we can avoid utopianism by following a similar strategy, comparing the accomplishments and ideals of that experiment with the feasible alternatives, not just with the perfect society. Neither my wife nor my country are off the hook for their failures, but I can avoid sinful censoriousness by being firm and merciful.

The other variety of utopianism we must avoid might be called the lure of the "third way." By this I mean to challenge not the motives but the conclusions of all those who set out determined not to embrace any existing solution but to invent an entirely distinct "biblical" option. Such an exercise may be useful for academic purposes, and it is possible that it may sometimes be fruitful to develop a vanguard with an entirely new vision. Further, it may be the case that all existing parties or programs are so tainted with evil that they must be rejected. But sometimes we must take sides with the lesser of two evils, especially if we have reason to believe that our tenaciously holding out for the *tertium quid* will ensure that the greater of two evils will carry the day and do much greater damage. Political realism requires the recognition that human sin may rule out any hope that our ideal program can ever be enacted or may ensure that if it is enacted, it will have no chance of achieving the desired ends. If the best is impossible to achieve, we should know how we can promote the better.

The growing fashion for language about Christian "transnationalism" strikes me as an evidence of this variety of utopianism. While our concerns should always transcend our national identity, they should never ignore it. My concern for the well-being of my own family does in a sense take precedence over my concern for your family. The two need not be mutually exclusive, though at times they might be.

It might be a nicer world if there were no international conflict, but that is not a world in which we live. Even on a planet populated only by regenerate sinners, there would be conflicts, as there are in the church today. My duty before God is not just to assert that there should be no conflict or that by recognizing this eternal truth I am therefore above the conflict; rather, it is my duty to ascertain what, given the existing state of affairs, my obligations under God to family, society, and nation might in fact be.

While I certainly concur that my first allegiance is to the kingdom of God, God in his providence has also made me a citizen of this country. Now what do I do? Claims on my person in this world must not override my duties to the kingdom, but my duties to the kingdom in fact may imply certain duties in this world and to this nation. If there are just wars (and I believe that there are), then there is no necessary conflict between my allegiance to God and to my country if I participate in such a war justly. Assertions about being members of a global community seem to be either a pious dodge around hard questions about temporal responsibilities or a cagey way of introducing the classical Anabaptist notion of two kingdoms without saying so or a way of saying that one is ashamed to be an American or some combination of the three. Whatever the root, it is an unfruitful line of reasoning.

SUCCUMBING TO POPULAR AGENDAS

While expressing a general warning regarding the lure of the "third way," I acknowledged that sometimes existing political options may possess some minor virtues and yet be so corrupted as to make involvement unwise. Whatever one's involvement, the Christian pursuing obedient political thought must not allow the issues to be defined in such a way as to deny essential Christian truths.

Since evangelicals are new to political thought, it is inevitable that we will pick up some dubious notions along the way and try to adapt them to suit our indubitably pure aims. In modern political thought, there is one fundamental notion that seems to me to be irredeemable and that we must not fail to discredit: the Marxist notion that human ideas and behavior are mere derivatives of power and profit.

The Christian insists that ultimate happiness and the source of meaning and authority are not contained or explained by political categories. But the dominant and increasingly accepted point of view in our time is that life is intrinsically and essentially political, that all activities and ideas have their source in the conscious or unconscious concern for temporal power or control. Defining the gospel as essentially a message about the powerful versus the powerless is one way of encouraging this heresy, as it reduces all spiritual conflict to a temporal conflict.

Rightly proclaimed, Christian thought asserts that politics is not ultimate but an expression of man's relationship with God and, at that, only one aspect of human culture through which we pursue our calling before God. We reject the thesis of the ultimacy of politics as a uniquely pernicious modern idolatry. This idolatry is worse than the mere worship of the state. One can worship the state and still believe in love, in sorrow, in beauty. But the modern ideology concludes that these deep human emotions are unreal, mere epiphenomena of politics. By reducing redemption to social liberation, theologians have taken the first step toward the abolition of man.

James V. Schall, in his book *Christianity and Politics*, writes that "The ultimate effect of Christianity on politics is a limiting one, one that frees man by removing from politics what politics cannot deliver. In this way, politics is left to be politics and not a substitute religion."

Not only do we say No to the thesis that politics is ultimate, but we also say No to the great hope that accompanies and gives drive to that thesis—namely, that we can build a perfect society. Yves Simon has said that if man were the highest being, politics would be the highest science. Similarly, earth would be the only place we could hope for paradise. With religion itself relativized, the age-old quest for a perfect society becomes the modern secular substitute for sanctification and glorification. The quest often assumes the rhetoric of remaking man, usually the "new socialist man." The phrase holds out the possibility that at last, here and now, humanity can enjoy its fullest possibilities. Since the new humanity is the goal of the revolution, the revolution inevitably becomes permanent, a necessary state of affairs until the new man emerges from the chrysalis of repression.

Christianity says No to the promise of remaking man—not because man does not need to be remade but because the very defects that require a remaking prevent man from being up to the task. Again, James V. Schall:

> If there is an abiding [sinful] nature of man, such as that found in the Christian tradition, then all men will expect a much more finite and confined goal to politics which will restore it to the tasks that are accomplishable in this world. The removal of all evil, greed, suffering, and disorder is not one such goal. The gradual, careful, imperfect improvement of our condition, through a realistic awareness of sin and envy and greed together with an awareness of the great capacities of reason and technique and

experience, is a generally feasible goal. And yet, this is to be always understood in the context of the human will, of the idea that things can get worse.

CONCLUSION

I have not said as much about democracy and the American experiment as I would have liked. This is in part because I feel that I have little new to contribute to what has been written already. It is also indicative of the need I believe we have of settling some procedural matters first. Instead of developing the outline of a political philosophy, I have tried to map out the pitfalls and the obstacles evangelicals encounter in such a pursuit.

In a recent discussion about the problems of South Africa with a colleague, I pointed out several potential problems with the strategy she was suggesting. "I don't believe Christians are obligated to worry about all of the details of statecraft," she insisted. Well, not all Christians. But Christians suggesting specific policies are. Good intentions count for something in God's eyes, but so does the wisdom that successfully translates those intentions into reality. Nourishing good intentions but ignoring the consequences of folly is a sort of hyper-Calvinism that says, "I'll worry about my motives and let God worry about picking up the pieces after I've made a mess of things."

Praise God that he does pick up the pieces when we err. But biblical obedience requires that we attempt to be as wise as serpents and as harmless as doves. Political thought is a prelude to political action, an arena of life and death. It is not the final life or the final death, and recognizing that will lend a unique dimension to our thought. At the last, God will pick up some pieces and give them new life, and he will smash some vessels into unrepairable pieces, fit only for destruction. But in the meantime, we have a humbler, if significant task.

An Evangelical Vision for American Democracy: An Anabaptist Perspective

Ronald J. Sider

Since we all reflect our history, I begin with mine. But that is not to suggest that we are helplessly imprisoned within our diverse traditions, that one tradition is as good or true as another, or that we owe ultimate loyalty to our religio-cultural heritage, however grand. I have only one passion in life: to submit every facet of my thinking and acting to Jesus Christ, whom I confess and worship as Lord and Savior.

But I came to know him as a farm boy raised in a devout Brethren in Christ home with strong Anabaptist, Wesleyan, and Pietist traditions. With family roots stretching back to persecuted sixteenth-century Swiss Anabaptists, I am not only formally affiliated with both Mennonite and Brethren in Christ congregations but also deeply convinced of the truth of the long Anabaptist belief that Christians made a tragic mistake when Constantine's offer of political power led to Christian justification of the sword.

Since high school, I have also been deeply involved with resurgent evangelicalism. Nurtured by InterVarsity Fellowship in college and graduate school, I found it natural to become active in the National Association of Evangelicals and the World Evangelical Fellowship. When a lack of concern for justice and peace among mainstream evangelicals frustrated and infuriated me, I turned for support not primarily to mainline Protestantism or Catholicism (although I am grateful for insights from both) but to a new generation of activist evangelicals ready to come together from diverse backgrounds (Wesleyan, Reformed, Southern Baptist, Anabaptist) to launch new projects such as Evangelicals for Social Action (ESA).

32

Deep involvement with people and movements bringing together these diverse evangelical traditions has been most stimulating. But it sometimes also poses problems. When faced with a task such as writing this essay, I have to decide whether to work as a Mennonite theologian or chairperson of ESA. I am a deeply committed Anabaptist pacifist, although not of the quietist variety. But most folk in ESA subscribe to the just-war tradition. I hope that much of what follows in this essay is common ground for both pacifist and "just war" evangelicals. But where the disagreement over war leads to divergent public policy choices, I have developed an Anabaptist perspective. Hence, my subtitle.

Since I have begun autobiographically, perhaps I may also be permitted to introduce my perspective on public policy in a democracy in a semiautobiographical fashion.

My vision for public life cuts across most of the political and ideological stereotypes. I believe that even on the basis of the just-war tradition, not only the use but also the very possession of nuclear weapons is immoral and unacceptable. I strongly endorse an immediate nuclear freeze; at the same time I reject abortion on demand. I want radical change in the foreign policy of Western nations toward the Two-Thirds World so that their influence sides with the poor masses rather than the affluent elite and transnational corporations, but I also want much tougher laws against drunken driving to reduce murder on our highways. I believe women have been seriously oppressed and I have endorsed the Equal Rights Amendment (though I would like a clause guaranteeing that it could not be used to support abortion on demand), but I also consider the strengthening of the family one of the most urgent concerns for current public policy and warmly approve of President Reagan's attempt to have parents notified when public agencies give minor children contraceptives. As a resident of inner-city Philadelphia for a number of years, I protest the persisting gross inequalities in education, housing, and jobs for blacks, Hispanics, and other minorities; at the same time I oppose the attempts of the homosexual and lesbian communities to use governmental processes to win social approval and legitimacy for their sexual lifestyles (although of course I defend the civil rights of homosexual sinners just as I defend the civil rights of adulterous sinners). I believe that we must protect the environment even if the result is slower economic growth; at the same time I applaud those citizens who use their economic votes to boycott companies whose advertising dollars support television programs crammed with sex and violence.

Some of these stances are popularly identified with liberal/left movements, others with conservative/right causes. It may be that I am simply a recalcitrant maverick or an inconsistent fool. But I hope not. I think there is reason in my madness. I have no commitment to ideologies of left or right. Obviously we have all been shaped by our past. But my goal is to transcend this historical and ideological baggage and allow Jesus Christ and biblical revelation to shape the stand I take on all issues of public policy.

As I do that, I find myself drawn to the kind of "consistent pro-life stand" just described. The rest of this essay is an attempt to outline and then illustrate the methodology of this approach.

THE NEED FOR A NEW VISION

Today, in the West, no dominant vision or widely accepted ethical values undergird and shape public life. Short-term economic or political self-interest rather than a common vision for justice and the common good determines most public decisions. The decay of traditional ethical values also profoundly affects the body politic as the family collapses and white-collar crime and corruption undermine business, law, medicine, and politics.

To the extent that there is any implicit guiding vision, it is a secular, materialistic one that virtually all religions would reject. Bernard Zylstra, principal of the Institute for Christian Studies in Toronto, puts it this way:

> The expansion of the production of material goods, and their consumption, is the highest good, the summum bonum of twentieth century civilization in Western Europe and North America. The increase in the gross national product (GNP) has become the chief end of human life, in comparison with which every other cultural purpose is secondary. The religion of production and consumption is the main cause of social disarray. For it permits the corporate industrial sector to encroach upon the legitimate social space of the family, marriage, education, the arts and the media. As a matter of fact, the very integrity of the state itself is endangered by the nearly uninhibited growth of the economic sector. . . . The origin of this extremely one-sided cultural development must be found in a specific notion of human progress that gained preeminence since the time of the eighteenth century enlightenment. Simply stated, that notion holds that progress consists in the unlimited fulfillment of human material needs.[1]

Zylstra is correct, I believe, in seeing the Enlightenment as a primary source for a number of contemporary problems. Abandoning

---

1. Zylstra, "The Bible, Justice and the State," in *Confessing Christ and Doing Politics*, ed. James W. Skillen (Washington: Association for Public Justice, 1982), pp. 52-55.

the notion of a transcendent Creator who is the source of normative ethical values, the Enlightenment grounded ethics in autonomous humanity. The result has been two centuries of ethical relativism. First Marx and then Freud and the sociologists argued that ethical values are merely the product of socio-cultural conditioning. Modern science, or at least a pseudo-scientific philosophy claiming the authority of science, has taught us that people are merely the product of a blind materialistic process governed by chance. If all life is merely the product of random materialistic processes, then people are simply complex machines, and ethical notions are merely subjective private feelings. The great mathematician and philosopher Bertrand Russell drew the proper conclusion. Those who have the best poison gas, he said, will determine the ethics of the future. Ethics is what those who, for the moment, hold the power say is right. The Marxist claim that whatever serves the interests of the party is good and true is merely one of the more candid evidences of the widespread ethical relativism rooted in the Enlightenment.

Evangelicals searching for a solid foundation for a new vision for public life believe that in the last two centuries the Enlightenment's ethical relativism has been tested by Western society and been found wanting. We also reject as inadequate the reasons given for abandoning the earlier Christian belief in a transcendent God who has intervened supernaturally in human history to reveal, among other things, ethical values that are an expression of his very nature.

Right at the heart of the modern rejection of historic Christian theism and its understanding of ethics is the view that those who accept the findings and implications of modern science can, for that reason, no longer believe in the supernatural elements of historical Christianity.[2] That means that one would have to reject the heart of historic Christian theism because at its very center stands the two colossal miracles of the Incarnation and Resurrection. Are the belief that God became flesh as the carpenter from Nazareth and the claim that Jesus was alive on the third day excluded by modern science? A host of philosophers and theologians from Hume and Kant to Ernst Troeltsch, Rudolph Bultmann, and Hans Küng have thought so. At the risk of seeming presumptuous, I want to argue that they were wrong.

Certainly the critical historical investigation that emerged in the eighteenth and nineteenth centuries in conjunction with the growth of modern science has helped us discover that many earlier miraculous tales were pure legend with no historical foundation. One can only be grateful

---

2. On this, see my "Miracles, Methodology, and Modern Western Christology," in *Sharing Jesus in the Two Thirds World*, ed. Vinay Samuel and Chris Sugden (Grand Rapids: Eerdmans, 1984), pp. 237-50; and Colin Brown, *Miracles and the Critical Mind* (Grand Rapids: Eerdmans, 1984).

for the more accurate historical knowledge that has emerged. But it is sheer intellectual confusion to suppose that more and more scientific information makes belief in miracles more and more intellectually irresponsible. Science simply tells us with greater and greater precision what nature regularly does. Or, to put it in Hume's terms, it simply describes observed regularity with greater and greater accuracy. In principle no amount of scientific information could ever tell us whether there might or might not be a God who transcends the natural order of observed regularity. Of course, if an all-powerful being who transcended nature happened to exist, then he could intervene in nature anytime he chose.

Evangelical Christians believe that has happened in the history of Israel and the life of Jesus of Nazareth. As a historian, I think that there is strong historical evidence for Jesus' life, death, and resurrection from the tomb. [3] It was because of the resurrection that the early church confessed that at the name of Jesus every knee should bow and every tongue confess that he is Lord of the universe, true God as well as true man. It is because of the resurrection that I believe the same thing and therefore also accept Jesus' teaching as the very Word of God. Jesus taught that the Old Testament is God's special revelation. The Christian church believes the same about the New Testament canon. Thus it is from God's Word, as disclosed in the canon of the Old and New Testaments, that I want to develop a new vision for public life.

METHODOLOGY

Next, I turn to the question of methodology. How do I propose to move from the Bible to concrete public policy proposals?

One of the particularly valuable emphases of Bruce Birch and Larry Rasmussen's book *Bible and Ethics in the Christian Life*[4] is the point that the Bible provides ethical guidance in a wide variety of ways. I want to focus on two ways that the Bible provides the foundation for my vision for public life (though in doing so, I do not deny the possibility of others): first, the biblical story supplies my basic perspective on all reality,[5] and, second, the Bible provides normative paradigms for such basic matters as the nature of economic justice.

---

3. On this, see, for example, George Eldon Ladd, *I Believe in the Resurrection* (Grand Rapids: Eerdmans, 1975), and my essay "Resurrection and Liberation," in *The Recovery of Spirit in Higher Education*, ed. Robert Rankin (New York: Seabury, 1980), pp. 170-71, and the works cited there.

4. Birch and Rasmussen, *Bible and Ethics in the Christian Life* (Minneapolis: Augsburg Publishing House, 1976).

5. By "biblical story," I do *not* mean something mythical or unhistorical; rather, I mean the central events of revelation history.

1. *The biblical story*. From creation to consummation, the Bible portrays free finite persons in dialogue with an infinite Creator. Made so they would be fulfilled only in free obedience to their Maker, persons have introduced enormous disorder into the entire created order through their proud attempts to place themselves rather than God at the center of reality.

Loving humanity too much to leave them alone in their self-destructive arrogance, God initiated a long redemptive process with Abraham and his descendants. His ultimate intention was to restore the broken beauty of creation to its original glory and wholeness. God repeatedly intervened in special ways so as to disclose to his chosen people an ever-broadening picture of the nature of shalom—a shalom that involved a complex web of right relationships between God and people, people and people, and people and nature. When the covenant people constantly ignored the invitation to shalom that God gave through the law and the prophets, a faithful remnant began to look for a time in the future when the reign of God would break decisively into history with the coming of God's Messiah, who would overcome all evil and usher in an eternal age of peace and justice.

Christians believe that the ancient Jewish hope was fulfilled in an unexpected way in the person and work of the carpenter from Nazareth. Claiming to be the Messiah sent to begin the messianic age, Jesus challenged every evil and injustice of the status quo. Repudiating the violent messianic hopes of his day, Jesus called his followers to love their enemies.[6] Rejecting the sexual discrimination of his time, which excluded women from theological investigation and prohibited them from appearing with men in public, Jesus treated women as equals. Ministering to the poor and oppressed and summoning his followers to do the same, Jesus challenged the economic establishment so thoroughly that it felt compelled to get rid of him. Rejecting the legalism of the religious leadership, he taught that God freely forgives even the worst of prodigals. He even claimed divine authority to forgive sinners. It is hardly surprising that he was crucified both as a blasphemous heretic and a dangerous social radical.

That would have been the end, except that God raised Jesus from the dead on the third day. It was the resurrection that convinced the early Christians that Jesus' messianic claim was valid and that the long-expected messianic kingdom had genuinely broken into history. As a result, the early church imitated Jesus' sweeping challenge to the status quo by offering the world a new society incarnating Jesus' kingdom values on

---

6. For a detailed exegetical argument for Jesus' nonviolence, see chapters 5-8 of *Nuclear Holocaust and Christian Hope* (Downers Grove, Ill.: InterVarsity Press, 1982), a book I wrote with Richard K. Taylor.

economic sharing, nonviolence, and the equality of all people. Women and slaves became persons. The rich engaged in economic sharing as there was need. Even as they were burned at the stake, they loved their enemies. The very character of the early Christian community was itself tangible evidence that the messianic age of peace and justice, so long expected by the prophets, had already begun.

However, it was also painfully clear that the old age of evil, injustice, and violence still persisted, even in the church to a certain degree. Jesus himself taught that the kingdom of God had begun with his life and work. He also said that the messianic kingdom of justice and peace would come in its fullness only at his second coming. Christians therefore look forward to a coming day, known only to God, when the risen Christ will return to complete his victory over all evil and injustice, when God's people will live forever in the presence of the risen Lord.

This biblical story shapes the Christian approach to public life in profound ways. For example, persons are not merely complex machines to be programmed for the good of the state. They are immeasurably valuable beings, so loved by their Creator that he suffered the hell of Roman crucifixion for them, free beings called to shape history along with God and neighbor, immortal beings whose ultimate destiny far transcends any passing political system. Public life is important because it shapes the social context in which people respond to God's invitation to live in right relationship with both himself and neighbor. But the state is not ultimate; it is accountable to the Creator of the galaxies, who is the ultimate source of the true and good.

2. *The Bible as the source of normative paradigms.* Next, I want to show how the Bible functions as the source of normative paradigms for developing a biblical understanding of any issue (e.g., economic justice or the family). Working out these paradigms is not a simple process. It is far more complex than selecting a few isolated proof texts relating to a given topic. If the entire biblical canon is God's Word, then one must carefully trace the treatment of a given issue throughout the entire development of biblical history. One must pay attention to the unique socioeconomic historical context of each scriptural passage and carefully weigh the different emphases in all genres of the biblical literature. Rigorous exegesis of each particular text, using the best biblical scholarship, is essential. Placing each passage within the broad sweep of biblical history is also important in order to understand the direction of its development and the full complexity of the biblical revelation.

Let us assume one wanted to develop a careful understanding of the biblical view of economic justice. One would need to start with the stewardship of creation outlined in Genesis, proceed through the complex traditions about the land in the Pentateuch, and carefully explore the prophetic denunciation of economic exploitation. One would need to examine the way Jesus' new messianic teaching and community ful-filled the prophetic hope for a new age of justice, probe the economic sharing in the early church, and understand the eschatological hope for a time when the tears and agony of the hungry and oppressed will be no more. Careful exegetical work would be necessary at every point.

But even after the detailed exegesis has been done and one has developed a comprehensive, synthetic overview of all the different, com-plementary perspectives on economic justice in all parts of the Bible, the task would only have just begun. Patriarchal society differed enormously from Roman Palestine and both differ even more substantially from the present global economy as viewed from Wall Street, Tokyo, or Moscow. Any naive attempt to transplant this or that specific aspect of biblical economic life into the twentieth century ignores the vast differences between the past and the present. The biblical paradigm must be faithfully applied, not blindly copied. As Chris Wright put it in the first issue of *Transformation*,

> It is assumed that cases and circumstances will differ, but if the principle is being properly applied, then it will be possible to recog-nize the pattern of the paradigm. In this sense, then, the social life of Israel [and the early church]—their laws and institutions—are to be taken as paradigmatic. We know that our circumstances and context differ greatly from those of ancient Israel [and the early church]. But as we study them we are able to form objectives and policies and to initiate action in our day which recognizably display the shape of the [biblical] paradigm.[7]

In order to develop a specific concrete proposal for today's public policy, grounded in the biblical paradigm, one must combine (in either one person or, normally, a team of scholars) a thorough understanding of the Scriptures and a sophisticated understanding of contemporary society. This requires socio-economic analysis, critical interaction with the methodology and findings of the various schools in the social sciences, and pragmatic testing to see if the specific proposals work. But pervading the entire process would be fundamental biblical values. The concrete public policy proposals would be judged to be biblical if the contempo-rary proposals clearly reflected the shape of the biblical paradigm.

I believe that every area of American public life would profit enor-mously if a generation of evangelical biblical scholars, social scientists, politicians, businessfolk, and professionals in all fields engaged in this

---

7. Wright, "The Use of the Bible in Social Ethics: Paradigms, Types and Eschatology," *Transformation* 1 (Jan.-March 1984): 17. See also his *Living as the People of God* (Leicester: InterVarsity Press, 1983).

kind of sweeping re-examination of law, education, health care, the economy, and the political process. I am not so naive as to suppose that there would ever be complete agreement. Christians cannot even agree on all aspects of the biblical story. There is bound to be even more disagreement in the development of the biblical paradigms on the family, sexuality, economic justice, peace, and the sacredness of human life. And when we arrive at specific public policy proposals that have been developed to reflect the biblical paradigms, there would be still more room for honest disagreement among equally devout, equally competent, equally honest Christians.

This is one reason why the church qua church should not constantly make pronouncements on specific political options. The church should articulate the biblical story and the biblical paradigms. At times, a body of believers in a congregation or denomination will feel clarity, agreement, and urgency on a matter. Then they, as a church, should say what they believe the specific political applications of the biblical story and paradigms are. More often this should be done by individual Christians in public life and by interdenominational Christian associations (e.g., Evangelicals for Social Action), whose specific purpose is the application of biblical data to the needs of current public policy. Such Christian associations and think tanks will always strive to develop clearly biblical proposals. They should always clearly articulate how they move from the normative biblical material to concrete contemporary proposals, but they can never claim divine authority for their specific suggestions. They will have to assume humbly that those who disagree with their specific proposals are also faithful Christians. Their hope will be that the ongoing dialogue will produce public policy proposals more faithful to the biblical paradigms.

Before proceeding to sketch an outline of the public agenda that I believe would flow from the Scriptures, I need to comment on some issues of my political philosophy that I think grow out of the biblical material.

BRIEF COMMENTS TOWARD A POLITICAL PHILOSOPHY

1. *Modest expectations.* Sin will persist in persons and social institutions until the eschaton. Therefore, it is crucial not to expect utopian results even from the best, most far-reaching structural changes in society. The Marxist dream of creating new persons through societal engineering is a dangerous illusion. Sin, unfortunately, is deeper than institutional structures. Only personal conversion through regenerating grace can truly transform egocentric personalities. To expect such change from public policy, however wise, is to exchange a biblical view of human nature for the naively optimistic secular humanism of the Enlightenment.

2. *Separation of church and state*. You might think that my agenda is beginning to sound like some theocratic attempt to use the state to impose evangelical Christianity on unwilling secular humanists. But I want to assure you that I believe deeply in the separation of church and state. (I am after all a descendant of those sixteenth-century Anabaptists who died by the thousands as martyrs for this belief long before the rest of Western society accepted their radical proposal.) The state should not promote or establish any religion or denomination.

Nor is the separation of church and state merely a pragmatic necessity in a pluralistic society. Religious faith by its very nature is a free response to God. It cannot be coerced. Throughout biblical history, we see a sovereign God constantly inviting persons into free dialogue with himself. He invites obedience but is astonishingly patient with those who decline the invitation. If the history of Israel tells us anything, it discloses how much space God gives people to reject his will and still continue to enjoy the created gifts of food, health, and life. Jesus' parable of the wheat and tares (Matt. 13:24ff.) makes it clear that God chooses to allow believers and nonbelievers to live and enjoy the world together until the end of history. Since God intends history to be the place where people have the freedom to respond or not respond to him, the state should not promote or hinder religious belief.

Sometimes, however, the separation of church and state is confused with the separation of public life from the ethical values grounded in religious faith. To make the charge that Jerry Falwell's political activity violates the separation of church and state as columnists in the *New York Times* have is absurd. He is only doing what the National Council of Churches and Jewish organizations have done for decades. His political proposals may be unwise or insufficiently biblical, but his proposing them hardly violates the separation of church and state.

Every major political decision and every debated public policy proposal finally depends on basic value judgments. These in turn are rooted in religious belief. Our political stance—not just on abortion and the nuclear arms race but on foreign policy toward Central America and the shape of the tax structure as well—is in part dependent on basic ethical commitments, whether conscious or unconscious. It would be as impossible as it would be immoral to try to separate public life from ethical values grounded in religious belief.

Every citizen is free to propose to the body politic a vision and a set of concrete public policy proposals for society that come from his or her most basic religious beliefs. In a pluralistic democratic society those proposals can become law only if a majority agree. If, as Christians believe, biblical revelation represents God's truth about the world and people, then public policy proposals made by Christians about economic justice or the family will with some frequency (though not always) make sense and appeal to many citizens, including some who do not share those religious foundations.

I want to make one other brief comment on the separation of church and state. Probably the best protection against political totalitarianism is the recognition that the state is not the ultimate source of value and law. If people in a society believe strongly that there exists a higher law grounded in God the Creator to which current legislation ought to conform and which citizens ought to obey even if that entails civil disobedience, totalitarianism will be held in check. But how can a secular state that is neutral toward religious conviction recognize the fact that governmental activity and law are finally accountable to God? In the United States we have done such things as appointing congressional chaplains, engraving coins with the slogan "In God We Trust," and approving state-sponsored prayer in the public schools. But all these things are inconsistent with the separation of church from state.

I believe that the responsibility for articulating this important protection against totalitarianism must be carried not by the state but by religious bodies and religious individuals in politics. Large numbers of devout politicians, inculcated by their churches and synagogues with a deep awareness that they are finally accountable to God, provide a far better way to preserve the societal understanding that the state is not ultimate than do inscriptions on coins. There is no reason why presidents, cabinet members, and congressional leaders could not frequently express in public their own personal conviction that no government is absolute and that the state's actions ought to conform to the norms and values grounded in the Creator. Frequent personal, albeit public, acknowledgment of this conviction would not violate the separation of church and state, and it could promote general acceptance of this crucial idea.

3. *Decentralized and global government.* There are both positive and negative reasons for decentralized government. Positively, biblical faith sees persons and families called to be coworkers with God in the shaping of history, responsible agents free to help mold the things that affect their lives. The more decentralized decision making is, the more this is possible. Negatively, the doctrine of human sin, which explains the dictum that power tends to corrupt and absolute power tends to corrupt absolutely, warns us not to centralize power. Decentralized decision making, even if it means a certain loss of efficiency, is in keeping with the biblical vision of persons as coshapers under God of their own history.

On the other hand, biblical faith also contains a powerful global thrust. The one sovereign of the entire universe has created all persons equal and cares equally for the total well-being of all. The selfish nationalism and narrow patriotism of modern nation-states find no justification in biblical thought. Therefore, Christians should strengthen global institutions such as the United Nations, but they should always do so in such a way as to encourage decision making at as local a level as is consistent with the demands of justice, order, and freedom.

4. *Democracy.* Both the positive and negative factors discussed in the previous section contribute to my conviction that the democratic political process (freedom of speech and assembly, universal suffrage, more than one political party in competition, etc.) is the political system most compatible with biblical values about the importance of the individual and the pervasiveness of sin. Genuine political democracy decentralizes political power more completely than any other form of government. As Reinhold Niebuhr never tired of pointing out, democracy is necessary precisely because people are sinful. At the same time, it is because each individual is of inestimable worth to God that every person should be free to help shape his or her political destiny.

5. *The importance of intermediate associations.* In the biblical paradigms of the state and the family, the individual is not nearly as absolute as in the dominant North American political philosophy that goes back to John Locke. Historian Rockne McCarthy, a member of the Association for Public Justice, puts it this way:

> The Enlightenment produced a liberal (individualist) tradition in which the rights of sovereign individuals are absolutized. This atomistic view of the sovereign individual became . . . a master assumption of American political thought. John Locke is recognized as the philosophical founder of the American liberal tradition. In his view of social reality, individuals are sovereign, and, therefore, inherently free of every associational relationship. From such a perspective all social entities are mere abstractions. . . . Thus only individuals have rights because only individuals are "real."[8]

This sovereignty of the individual can be seen in recent legal decisions that make the mother the sole determinant of whether the offspring of a husband and wife should be aborted and deny that parents must be informed when their teenagers receive contraceptives. A biblical perspective would pay far more attention to the fact that individuals are members of intermediate associations (such as the family and the church or synagogue) that also have rights and responsibilities that the state should recognize and preserve. The biblical paradigm of the family would suggest that the right of parents to know about and exercise responsibility for the fact that their minor teenagers are receiving contraceptives overrides other valid concerns.

---

8. McCarthy, in *Confessing Christ and Doing Politics*, pp. 66-67.

6. *What are the ethical values that should be legislated?* From the perspective of biblical faith, racism in the rental of housing on the one hand, and adultery on the other, are equally sinful. Does that mean that there should be laws against both? If not, why not?

I want to argue that the state should not legislate criminal penalties for breaking biblical ethical norms except where those infractions violate the rights of others. The churches, of course, should have their own internal mechanisms for dealing with sins such as lying, adultery, and racist attitudes.

But persons should be free to harm themselves and consenting associates (with, for instance, adultery or excessive use of alcohol) without facing legal penalties, as long as they do not harm others or infringe on their rights. Therefore, laws against racial prejudice in the sale or rental of housing which guarantee that the rights of others are not violated are appropriate, whereas laws making adultery a civil offence are not.

Obviously this general principle does not solve all problems. Alcoholic mothers or fathers and adulterous spouses harm their families as well as themselves. That injury, however, extends to a relatively small number of people who have a special commitment to each other. Racial discrimination in housing, on the other hand, affects a whole class of people without any consent on their part. The very nature of the family entails an implied consent that all members share both the positive and negative aspects of family life. This mutual commitment, and the family's existence as an intermediate association independent of the state, means that the state should not intervene in the family. There are exceptions of course, in extreme situations such as serious physical abuse of the spouse or children or denial of medical treatment necessary for survival. Normally citizens should be free to break accepted (or biblical) ethical norms without legal penalty except where such infractions violate the rights of others.

The fact that the state does not legally prohibit adultery or homosexuality or divorce does not mean, however, that it cannot offer incentives for a lifestyle or an ethical stance that it considers helpful for society. The state should not make practicing homosexuality a crime, and it should uphold the civil rights of homosexuals so that they have access to jobs and housing. But that does not mean that the state must remain neutral with regard to homosexual and heterosexual lifestyles. The state should decide not to sanction homosexual relationships with civil marriage. The state should refuse to pass legislation whose basic purpose is the legitimatization of homosexuality. Similarly, the state should, through its tax laws, make heterosexual marriage more advantageous financially than cohabitation.

SOME PROPOSALS FOR PUBLIC POLICY

1. A *biblically balanced agenda*. If Christians in politics want to claim
that Christ is head of their political life, then they must adopt a political
agenda that reflects the balance of concerns suggested by biblical revelation. That perhaps is the best test of whether one's political agenda is
shaped by ideological bias or Christian faith.

If the Scriptures repeatedly tell us that God is very concerned about
justice for the poor, then it is fundamentally—that is, *biblically*—unacceptable for Christians to start Moral Majority and decide that justice
for the poor will not be a major item of concern.[9] If the Scriptures tell us
that human life is almost infinitely precious and that the family is a
central divinely willed intermediate institution in society, then it is fundamentally unacceptable to endorse a political platform that ignores or
weakens societal concern for life and family. And if biblical faith emphasizes the importance of both freedom and justice, it will not do to support
institutions and trends that sacrifice one to the other.

It is ironic that the same people who (sometimes rightly) charge
ecumenical church leaders with stressing justice and de-emphasizing
democratic freedoms so often produce programs that sacrifice justice for
the sake of freedom. For example, one looks in vain for any central
emphasis on justice in the several drafts of the proposed Peace, Freedom
and Security Studies Program of the National Association of Evangelicals. And why does the Institute on Religion and Democracy fail to
focus as much energy on injustice in the Philippines (under Marcos) as
on restrictions on freedom in Nicaragua (under the Sandinistas)? In fact,
would it not make sense for organizations to do joint studies in which
countries such as Nicaragua and the Philippines were compared with
each other with an equal concern for both justice and freedom?

To insist on a biblically balanced agenda is not to ignore the reality
of historical *kairoi*. At a given moment, history is ripe for a new initiative.
Some imbalance demands redress. And we cannot do everything at once.
Precisely at such a time, however, it is essential to keep our eye fixed on
the North Star of biblical balance lest we lurch from one extreme to
another. We also need to remember that Jesus and the prophets were
usually challenging and resisting cultural trends rather than applauding
the dominant consensus. Those who were radicals in the sixties and are
now neoconservative in the eighties ought to ask themselves who is
setting the agenda. If justice for the poor was a biblical imperative in the

---

9. In an interview, Jerry Falwell explicitly said, "We could never bring
the issue of the poor into Moral Majority. . . . We just have to stay away from
helping the poor" (*Christianity Today*, 4 September 1981, p. 27).

sixties, it ought to be central to any faithful Christian political movement in the eighties. In fact, precisely at a time when the larger American society seems to want to ignore the poor at home and abroad, Christians stubbornly committed to a biblical agenda should place even greater emphasis on this area (without thereby neglecting freedom, family, or the sanctity of life). A biblically shaped agenda will lead us to say what most needs to be said rather than what attracts the largest audience.

In order to strive for what I believe is a biblical balance, therefore, I will deal both with issues of great concern to liberal activists (i.e., issues of economic justice and global peace) and also with issues rightly emphasized by conservatives (e.g., the family and the sacredness of human life).

2. *Economic justice.* The starting point of all biblical thinking on economics is that Yahweh is sovereign.[10] God alone is the absolute owner of all things, and he intends the earth's resources to be used for the benefit of all.

The Bible rejects all notions of any absolute private ownership of property. As such passages as the Jubilee text in Leviticus 25 indicate, the right of families to have the resources to earn their own way is a higher right than the property rights of the person who has purchased the land. This does not deny all notions of private ownership. Limited private ownership is the biblical pattern when it is understood as the stewardship of resources for the good of the family and the neighbor in an obedient response to God as the ultimate owner. Centralizing all economic power in the state through public ownership of all the means of production does not correspond to the biblical paradigm, and it almost certainly guarantees totalitarianism. For that reason, I am opposed to socialism.

Extremes of wealth and poverty are displeasing to the God revealed in the Bible. The Old Testament contains institutionalized structures (rather than mere charity) that, if followed, would have systematically prevented or reduced the gap between rich and poor. Although they do not suggest a wooden, legalistic equality of consumption, the biblical patterns of economic sharing in both testaments move away from extremes of wealth and poverty. Probably nothing is clearer in the Scriptures than God's special concern for and identification with the poor, the weak, and the oppressed.

I am a theologian, not a political scientist or economist, so I will not try to suggest a detailed economic program or a political strategy for implementing the biblical paradigm. I do, however, want to suggest the general direction I believe is required. Economic justice for the poor, both domestically and internationally, must be a top concern for any

---

10. For a more extensive statement, see chapters 3-6 of my *Rich Christians in an Age of Hunger: A Biblical Study*, rev. ed. (Downers Grove, Ill.: InterVarsity Press, 1984).

Christian politician who wants to make any claim that Christ is Lord of his or her political life. It is intolerable that the poorer sections of society pay the social costs of reducing inflation. A fundamental redistribution of power and resources (including education, productive capabilities, and capital) is necessary.

Internationally, a fundamentally different approach to foreign policy is essential. The Scriptures totally reject any idea of private ownership that suggests that the West has a right to enjoy solely for itself all the natural resources and abundance that our particular geography and history place in our hands. Even if it is costly, even if it should lower our standard of living, the first priority of American foreign policy toward the Two-Thirds World should be the advancement of democracy and freedom and the reduction of hunger and poverty through the promotion of programs that enable the poorer half of the world's people to earn their own way.

3. *The family.* In the biblical paradigm, the family is one of the central, divinely willed intermediate societal associations. A lifelong marital covenant between one man and one woman is the Christian norm. The family, not the state, is the primary institution for rearing children. Christians must resist the growing tendency of the state to usurp the role of the family.

It is generally acknowledged that the contemporary family is in trouble. Primary responsibility for revitalizing and renewing the biblical vision of the family and of sexuality lies, of course, not with the state and the media but with religious institutions. But the state and the media do have a significant secondary role. Surely it is not too much to ask for TV, radio, and film to portray models of wholesome families and sexual fidelity more often than they currently do. If the only artistically excellent scripts to arrive on the desks of the small elite who control the content of the media always portray sexual promiscuity, broken homes, petty parents, and rebellious children, then the small circle of artists and producers needs to be expanded. Economic pressure on the advertisers by means of consumer boycotts is one way to begin. All legislation, including tax structures, should help create a social and financial climate conducive to strong, responsible families, and lifelong marriage covenants. Parents, not the state, have the basic responsibility for helping teenagers avoid pregnancy.

Christian organizations and think tanks need to do much more in order that the public can be given some clear public policy options for the government and the media that would strengthen rather than further weaken the family.

4. *The sacredness of human life.* Every person is created in the image of God. Since God desires all to be saved (1 Tim. 2:4), so much so that he sent his Son to die "as a ransom for all" (1 Tim. 2:6), every person

in the world is immeasurably valuable. The value and worth of each person are totally independent of his or her social usefulness or ability to experience a certain standard of self-fulfillment. Obviously a host of difficult questions, including euthanasia and genetic engineering, demand attention. But I shall concentrate on one issue that is particularly difficult and controversial—namely, abortion. I believe the U.S. Supreme Court made a fundamental mistake in 1973 when it allowed abortion on demand.

Developments in the past ten years have already provided some indication of the dangerous road that could lead from abortion to scientific experimentation on fetuses that will be aborted to infanticide to quietly exterminating the very old and the very deformed. We must at the very least reject abortion as a convenient method of birth control and permit it only in case of rape, incest, or danger to the physical life of the mother. Abortion on demand is immoral and must be rejected. Biologically, the fetus is obviously human life. Since there is no extensive explicit biblical teaching on whether or when the fetus becomes a human being, it is better to err on the side of caution. [11]

I am aware of the problems of this position, but I believe it presents fewer difficulties and dangers than the alternatives. Certainly the Christians who adopt this stance must actively support pregnancy advisory centers and adoption programs for those unmarried women (especially teenagers) who become pregnant. It is to the credit of the Christian Action Council, the major evangelical antiabortion lobby, that its members have done this in a major way.

5. *Peacemaking in a nuclear age.* Finally, I turn to the arms race and my most radical proposals. Most Christians stand within the just-war tradition. I agree with those who think that if one applies the criteria of the just-war tradition to the question of nuclear weapons, one must reject not only the use of strategic nuclear weapons (and also tactical nuclear weapons, since their use would probably escalate to strategic weapons) but also their very possession. [12] That was the conclusion of the vast majority of Christian leaders from all parts of the world who met in Sweden for an international conference 20-24 April 1983. If they are correct, Christians must demand not only an immediate freeze on all testing and deployment of nuclear weapons but also total nuclear disarmament within some short specified time.

---

11. See Part I of my forthcoming book *What Does It Mean to Be Pro-Life?* (Downers Grove, Ill.: InterVarsity Press, 1987), which deals with both the biblical/theological and public policy aspects of abortion.

12. On this, see chapter 4 of *Nuclear Holocaust and Christian Hope*; see also *Peace and War: A Debate about Pacifism* (Nottingham: Grove Books, 1985), which I wrote with Oliver O'Donovan, for a discussion of the just war and pacifist position.

Personally I believe we need to go even further. Christians must be prepared to act according to our own ethical tradition regardless of what the Soviet Union does. If we argue that we may even go so far as commit what the just-war tradition says is murder in order to protect ourselves from Soviet totalitarianism, then the ethical relativism of Marxist thought has already conquered us. If the possession of nuclear weapons is immoral, then we must abandon them no matter what the Kremlin does.

But this stance does not require unilateral disarmament if that means the abandonment of all forms of defense. We should be ready to die to defend democratic freedom, although we should not murder hundreds of millions of people to protect ourselves from Soviet totalitarianism. We should seriously explore the possibility of civilian-based defense as an alternative national policy for defending democratic values.[13] In the last section of our book *Nuclear Holocaust and Christian Hope*, Dick Taylor and I have spelled out how the tactics of Gandhi and Martin Luther King, Jr., could be adopted by a whole society for national self-defense. Such a proposal may seem politically naive, but if we cannot or will not negotiate bilateral disarmament, the only alternatives are civilian-based defense or nuclear holocaust.

For millennia humanity has sought security through violence. Almost all societies have hoped that state-of-the-art weapons would deter aggressive neighbors. Sometimes it has worked for short intervals, but it has seldom done so for long.

Ever more sophisticated technology has provided ever more deadly weapons. Clubs gave way to longbows, chariots to tanks, and cannon to nuclear missiles and lasers. Very seldom, and never for long, did the new weapons improve anyone's security. Ever more deadly weapons merely guaranteed that the next battle would destroy even more people.

Today we stand at the end of that long violent road littered with the mangled bodies of our best sons and daughters. Today state-of-the-art weapons enable us to destroy the planet. Every new generation of nuclear weapons shortens the fuse on the nuclear trigger and reduces our security. The best insights of conventional wisdom are in reality suicidal madness. We are at an impasse.

The only way to avoid disaster is to take a different path. Security through violence has never worked well; it will not work at all today. King was right: "Today the choice is no longer between violence and nonviolence. It is either nonviolence or nonexistence."[14]

For the first three centuries the early Christians rejected the violence of war—as well as abortion and capital punishment. They did so

---

13. See Gene Sharp, *The Politics of Nonviolent Action* (Boston: Porter Sargent, 1973) and the bibliography in *Nuclear Holocaust and Christian Hope*, pp. 301-2.

14. King, *Stride toward Freedom* (New York: Harper, 1958), p. 224.

because they believed that Jesus' summons to love their enemies was a daring call to reject lethal violence as the way to security, peace, and justice. I believe Jesus' costly invitation to suffer rather than kill is the only genuine alternative to the path that leads to nuclear holocaust. If North American society were to dare to try such a policy, it would undoubtedly pay a heavy price. But it would also lead the way out of the impasse that will likely end in global suicide.

I am quite aware that my proposal for civilian-based defense sounds incredibly naive in the realistic world of power politics, so brilliantly described by people such as Henry Kissinger. But such realism and the wisdom of power politics are at least as insane. They have brought us to the brink of annihilation. Is it not time to consider an alternative seriously?

Niebuhrian realists, to be sure, will denounce all nonviolent alternatives even when they are grounded in the teaching of Jesus and a biblical view of human sinfulness. Reinhold Niebuhr repeatedly said that Jesus taught a clear uncompromising ethic of total opposition to violence. But Niebuhr then explicitly rejected this nonviolent approach to enemies as an impossible ideal in a fallen world.[15] I can understand how Christians with a low view of biblical authority and the person of Christ can adopt such a position, but I find it puzzling in the case of people who affirm the infallibility of the Scriptures and a historic Christology.

If Jesus Christ is not only God's final revelation to us but also God in the flesh, how can a central element of his teaching be set aside in the way Niebuhr does? John Howard Yoder's question is pertinent: "What becomes of the meaning of incarnation if Jesus is not normative man? If he is man but not normative, is this not the ancient ebionitic heresy? If he be somehow authoritative but not in his humanness, is this not a new gnosticism?"[16]

Right at the heart of New Testament faith is the claim that the long-expected messianic kingdom actually broke into history in the person and work of Jesus in such a decisive way that it is now possible by grace for Christians to live the radical values the Messiah taught. To deny this is to reject a central element of Jesus' good news of the kingdom. (See further my brief excursus on the neglect of sanctifying grace in Niebuhr's rejection of pacifism, pp. 52-53 herein.)

To be sure, Christians should not suppose that fallen humanity will be able as fully as regenerate believers to live Jesus' ethic. (If Jesus is God's final revelation to all people, then of course they ought to; their failure is the measure of their sinful rebellion.) But Christians will not

---

15. See, for instance, Niebuhr's "Why the Christian Church Is Not Pacifist," in *Christianity and Power Politics* (New York: Scribner's, 1946), p. 8.
16. Yoder, *Politics of Jesus* (Grand Rapids: Eerdmans, 1972), p. 22.

therefore conclude that they ought to delay living Jesus' ethic until non-Christians do so. That is to turn New Testament ethics, grounded in the good news of the kingdom, on its head. Rather, Christians will by grace model now what they know all people will live when the kingdoms of this world become the kingdom of our Lord.

Meanwhile it is appropriate for Christians to propose concrete next steps that believers and nonbelievers can both accept in order to move the total society a little closer to kingdom values. And Christians will sometimes propose arguments advocating such steps that appeal to the presuppositions and long-term self-interest of nonbelievers. At this level, too, they will be vitally concerned for realism and effectiveness. But they will never allow "realism" to replace Jesus as the norm for their activity. They will never make the highest ethical possibilities for nonbelievers the norm for their own activity in public life. Even when for strategic reasons they appeal to the ethical values of non-Christians, the ethical foundation of all their own activity in public life will always be Jesus and biblical revelation. [17]

In order to survive, public life requires radical transformation—not just in the United States but around the world. I am quite aware that my proposals will not become accepted political policy in the immediate future. Since in the United States the major political parties are parties of consensus, fundamentally new political ideas must initially find a home outside their ranks. This is happening today in a significant segment of the Christian church.

One can see the early stages of a potentially significant new "pro-life" political coalition beginning to take shape within the churches. The U.S. Catholic bishops have taken a strong stand against abortion and the nuclear arms race and in favor of the family and justice for the poor. Evangelicals for Social Action is just one small piece of what is probably a major block of evangelical Protestants open to a similar "consistent pro-life" agenda. Some of the mainline Protestant denominations are having second thoughts about their strong defense of abortion. And in secular circles one sees liberal activists such as Nat Hentoff attacking abortion. [18]

But we will need more than dreams and strategies for new political coalitions. In his brilliant Harvard doctoral dissertation *Revivalism and Social Reform*,[19] historian Timothy Smith has shown how the North

17. To claim, as Neuhaus seems to, that this kind of appeal to revelation is a fundamentalist, pietistic subjectivism that must be abandoned (see, for example, pp. 36-37 of his book *The Naked Public Square* [Grand Rapids: Eerdmans, 1984]) is to reject Jesus' lordship over the Christian's political life.

18. See Hentoff, "The Awful Privacy of Baby Doe," *Atlantic Monthly*, January 1985, pp. 54-62.

19. Smith, *Revivalism and Social Reform* (New York: Harper, 1957). See also, Donald W. Dayton, *Discovering an Evangelical Heritage* (New York: Harper, 1976).

American tradition of religious revivals played a major role in the development of the abolitionist movement against slavery.

Today, more and more evangelicals are beginning to talk about a similar movement. We dream about a peace revival sweeping the North American churches. We dream of millions of people experiencing or returning to a living personal relationship with God in Christ. We dream of millions of Christians discovering the biblical God of shalom, the God who invites the people of our unjust, polluted, and endangered planet to return to right relationships with the Creator, other people, and nature. We dream of a vast movement of Christians so captivated by the biblical vision of shalom that they join other people of good will in a sustained campaign for economic justice, stable families, an end to racial and sexual discrimination, the protection of the environment and the sacredness of human life, and global peace. I expect to see a major part of my vision for public life become a reality only if the Sovereign of history astonishes our secular society with a mighty peace revival.

Even then, of course, we would not have utopia. Politicians and preachers would still often be petty, selfish, and misguided. Societal institutions would still need restructuring. But we might at least wend our way through the next two decades, the most dangerous in human history, without experiencing global disaster. That itself would be enough. That itself would confirm my belief that the best clue to the nature of reality is contained in the biblical story about the God of shalom who became flesh in the Peacemaker from Nazareth.

EXCURSUS ON THE NEGLECT OF SANCTIFYING GRACE IN NIEBUHR'S REJECTION OF PACIFISM

Reinhold Niebuhr's classic essay has the title "Why the *Christian Church* Is Not Pacifist." He is—or at least ought to be—talking about Jesus' new Spirit-filled, messianic community. With the early Christians, I believe that the new age has truly broken into this old order. I believe Jesus' new messianic community can, by the power of the Holy Spirit, begin to incarnate now the radical norms of Jesus' new kingdom. I do not believe in education and disarmament conferences, although both have value. I believe in the transforming power of the Holy Spirit.

In Niebuhr's thought, the church is a weak, pale reflection of the Spirit-filled New Testament community of transformed believers, the kingdom is entirely transcendent and future, and the Holy Spirit is almost nonexistent. Does this not smack of liberalism? In his classic work *Moral Man and Immoral Society*, Niebuhr argues that individuals are less selfish, wicked, and immoral than social groups. Therefore, he does not believe that any social groups, even the church, can practice in society as a whole Jesus' ethic of love for the enemy. But that is to deny both the practice and teaching of the first Christians. In the power of the Holy Spirit, they demonstrated a costly love both within and outside the church. The world could only utter in amazement, "Behold how they love one another." In the Spirit's power, it is possible to apply Jesus' ethic in the home and the marketplace, the church and the public arena. Again and again, the apostle Paul and the other apostles taught that Christians could and should live in the Spirit, not in the flesh. Why? Because the new messianic kingdom had begun. God has delivered Christians from the dominion of the old age and "transferred us to the kingdom of his beloved Son" (Col. 1:13, RSV). In the power of the Holy Spirit, the down payment and guarantee of the kingdom's presence, Christians can live lives that are dramatically different from their surrounding immoral societies.

In his classic essay, Niebuhr also operates with an inadequate concept of grace:

> Grace is conceived as "justification," as *pardon rather* than power, as the forgiveness of God, which is vouchsafed, to man despite the fact that he never achieves the full measure of Christ. . . . In this doctrine of forgiveness and justification, Christianity measures the full seriousness of sin as a permanent factor in human history.*

This appears dangerously close to an excuse for Christians to continue in sin that grace may abound. Certainly Christians in this life never attain earthly perfection. But they do, if Paul is not entirely mistaken, experience radical renewal by the power of the Holy Spirit. Therefore they should and can live according to the values of the new messianic kingdom.

Paul never argued that because sin still lingers in the Christian, it is therefore acceptable to fornicate, lie, and steal. Why then would anyone

---

*Niebuhr, "Why the Christian Church Is Not Pacifist," p. 3. I am quite aware that Niebuhr, in the sentence just before the one quoted, recognizes grace as "the power of righteousness which heals the contradiction within our hearts." But he does not maintain Paul's balance of these two aspects of grace. Later (pp. 18ff.), Niebuhr asks whether Galatians 2:20 means primarily justification or renewal. He says it means both, but then he proceeds to emphasize only the former. A scholarly study of Paul's doctrine of *dikaiosune* makes it quite clear that for Paul grace means both forgiveness and Spirit-empowered renewal in equal measure (see J. A. Ziesler, *The Meaning of Righteousness in Paul: A Linguistic and Theological Enquiry* [Cambridge: Cambridge University Press, 1972]). This balanced doctrine of grace, supports not Niebuhr's pessimistic rejection of pacifism but rather a Spirit-filled optimism about the possibility of Christian nonviolence.

argue that the awful persistence of sin even in Christians justifies our ignoring the New Testament's call to love our enemies? Certainly that is difficult. Certainly we will often fail. But surely we should not excuse or justify that sinful failure. Rather, with Paul we should repeat the glorious promise that in Christ all things are indeed possible. Biblical pacifism is not grounded in a naive, optimistic view of human nature but rather in a fully biblical affirmation of regenerating sanctifying grace.

The Bible, Politics, and Democracy: What Does Biblical Obedience Entail for American Political Thought?

James W. Skillen

For those who take biblical revelation seriously as the authoritative word from God for their lives, all of life must be viewed in its light. Political life cannot be excepted. The big questions among such people are not about *whether* the Bible has something to say to politics, but about *what* the Bible says and about *how* to interpret those texts in the context of our times.

The Association for Public Justice was formed for the purpose of trying to pose and answer some of the most important questions about the Bible and contemporary politics in order to guide responsible political action. My thinking has been shaped in the context of those associational efforts for more than a decade, so the following remarks should be taken not as peculiarly my own but as the fruit of serious communal reflection and action among one group of Christians.[1] One of the greatest concerns of the Association for Public Justice is to promote dialogue with others, especially with other Christians, about the nature of political responsibility. In that spirit, this paper should be taken as a plea for continued discussion rather than as a finished word to be accepted as it stands.

---

1. See my book *Christians Organizing for Political Service* (Washington: Association for Public Justice Education Fund, 1980); *Confessing Christ and Doing Politics*, ed. James W. Skillen (Washington: APJ Education Fund, 1982); and "Justice for All," a position paper published by the Association for Public Justice, 806 15th St. N.W., #218, Washington, D.C. 20005).

BIBLICAL REVELATION IS NORMATIVE

At the start I wish to emphasize a distinction between "norm" and "form." Accepting the Bible as "normative" means to accept its authority as entailing standards, statutes, laws, and guiding judgments that call for a creative human response to God's will. The Bible is a "hearing and doing" book; we should *act* in creative, stewardly obedience when we *hear* God's commandments. This stands in contrast to the "seeing and copying" attitude of formalistic idealism whether in its ancient or modern varieties. I find no basis in the Scriptures for assuming that God possesses an ideal form of government that we ought to be able to discover by rational and biblical reflection. As Christians we should not be *looking* for some eternal *form* of the state so we can use it as a model, but rather trying to *hear* what God's command of justice requires of us so we can *do* justice in the historical context in which we find ourselves.[2]

There is much more to biblical revelation, of course, than mere commands and statutes for human beings to obey. I am not suggesting that the Bible is primarily or only a rule book for living. The Bible reveals God and the meaning of his covenants with his creatures, showing the purpose of creation, exposing human sinfulness, and proclaiming the judgment and redemption of all things in Jesus Christ. The Bible is an all-encompassing testimony to the meaning and destiny of the world. Thus, we should read the Bible to understand how the historical unfolding of God's revelation, from Torah to the gospel, illumines the path on which we are now walking between the times of Christ's first and second comings. We should try to understand the connection between the Old and New Testaments—a connection explained by the Gospels and the epistles themselves (Matt. 5:17-48; John 7:14-29; 8:31-59; Acts 6:8–7:60; Gal. 3:1-29; 5:1-26; Heb. 8–11). These biblical texts open the way to an understanding of God's authoritative standards for our responsibility today (see, for example, Deut. 7:1-5; 11:1-7, 18-23; 1 Sam. 16:1-13; Jer. 21:11-12; 22:13-17; Mic. 3:1-4; Matt. 22:34-46; 23:1-12; Rom. 12:17–13:10; 1 Cor. 6:1-11; Rev. 5:1-14; 15:1-4).[3]

---

2. See H. Evan Runner, *Scriptural Religion and Political Task* (Toronto: Wedge Publishing Foundation, 1974); S. G. De Graff, *Promise and Deliverance*, 4 vols., trans. H. Evan Runner (St. Catharines, Ont.: Paideia Press, 1977-80); and my essay "Politics, Pluralism, and the Ordinances of God," in *Life Is Religion: Essays in Honor of H. Evan Runner*, ed. Henry Vander Goot (St. Catharines, Ont.: Paideia Press, 1981), pp. 195-206.

3. See Henry Vander Goot, *Interpreting the Bible in Theology and the Church* (New York: Edwin Mellen Press, 1984); Albert M. Wolters, *Creation Regained: Biblical Basics for a Reformational Worldview* (Grand Rapids: Eerdmans, 1985); Paul Marshall, *Thine Is the Kingdom* (Grand Rapids:

As will become clear in what follows, my acceptance of biblical authority and my interpretation of biblical texts does not lead to an absolutizing of certain Old Testament experiences, laws, and customs as the "model" for a contemporary state. Nor do I think the Bible allows for any idealization of the U.S. Constitution as a "revelatory" document. Nor do I think that biblical prophecy allows one to fit the modern states of Israel and the United States into a grand scheme for the end times in order to concoct foreign policy out of a supposedly special knowledge (gnosis) of God's hidden will.

BIBLICAL REVELATION AND THE UNFOLDING OF MODERN HISTORY

First, then, some comments about the meaning of biblical revelation for the historical context of modern politics.

Earthly politics, just like every other part of human life, unfolds before the face of God. Nothing has a life or meaning of its own apart from God. Biblical revelation begins and ends by referring all things to the sovereign God who is Creator and Lord, the one who has everything to do with politics in all ages, the one who has unveiled his glory in his only Son—the King of kings and Lord of lords.

> Great and marvelous are your deeds,
>   Lord God Almighty.
> Just and true are your ways,
>   King of the ages.
> Who will not fear you, O Lord,
>   and bring glory to your name?
> For you alone are holy.
>
> All nations will come
>   and worship before you,
> for your righteous acts have been revealed.
>
> REVELATION 15:3-4, NIV

The law, the prophets, and the psalms placed human politics in the context of the anticipation of One who would come as the Prince of Peace, the Just King, the Righteous Lord, the Perfect Judge, the Mighty God (Isa. 9:6-7; 40:9-11; Jer. 23:6; Pss. 82:8; 98:4-9). When Christ was with us on earth, he announced that "All things have been committed to

---

Eerdmans, 1986); Meredith G. Kline, *The Structure of Biblical Authority* (Grand Rapids: Eerdmans, 1972); Bernard Zylstra, "The Bible, Justice and the State," in *Confessing Christ and Doing Politics*, pp. 39-53; and Richard Mouw, *Politics and the Biblical Drama* (Grand Rapids: Eerdmans, 1976).

me by my Father" (Matt. 11:27). "All authority in heaven and on earth has been given to me" (Matt. 28:18). Jesus Christ came to fulfill the rule of his Father over the whole earth (Luke 4:1-21; 1 Cor. 15:20-28; Phil. 2:5-11; Col. 1:15-20; Rev. 19:1-16). If one accepts Jesus Christ as the promised Messiah, then one cannot escape his political claims.

But how did Christ fulfill the law and the prophets? How did he place himself in relation to Israel as God's chosen but now exiled people? What kind of kingdom did he come to establish? How did he answer the disciples' question about whether now was the time when he would "restore the kingdom to Israel"? (Acts 1:6) What was his political agenda?

According to the New Testament writers, the period between Christ's first and second comings is a time of great patience and long-suffering on God's part. God is not willing that any should perish, and so the call goes out to the whole world to repent and to believe the gospel of his kingdom (Mark 1:15; Acts 1:7-8; 2 Pet. 3:9). During this time, which is the time in which we still live, Jesus did not ask his disciples to administer any kind of forceful, political separation of non-Christians from Christians. Instead, his followers were commanded to love their enemies, to look after the welfare of others (including those who do evil to them), to pray for God's will to be done on earth as in heaven, and to leave in God's hands the responsibility for any final separation of believers and unbelievers (Matt. 5:38-48; 6:10; 26:51-54; Luke 3:15-17; Rom. 12:20; Phil. 2:4; Rev. 5:1-14).

The parable of the wheat and the tares (Matt. 13:24-30) is very important here. In the Gospel's context this parable prohibits any idealizing of ancient Israel and the longing for a return to a separate, pre-exile state for God's people. It holds out no hope for a "Christian state" in which Christians are organized into a separate political existence from which all non-Christians are removed. The "tares" (enemies of the kingdom) are to enjoy the same rain and sunshine, the same care and fertilizer, as the "wheat" (followers of Christ) so long as both are in this world together. This is a picture of God's kingdom during a time of both trials and grace—a time when both the redeemed and the unredeemed enjoy God's care and patience while the call goes out to repent.

A Christian view of justice, a Christian view of modern politics, I believe, should be built on this understanding of God's gracious patience during this age. It would not be *Christian* justice for Christians to enjoy some political privilege denied to others. A just state, a just world, is one in which all citizens enjoy the same civil rights and public care. Christian politics cannot be the church's attempt to control the state for its own well-being; Christian politics cannot be constituted by typical interest-group competition to make sure that Christians get their way while others have to fend for themselves.

The people of God, the followers of Christ, will remain dispersed throughout all the kingdoms of this world until the second coming—until the kingdom of God comes in its fullness. Political communities governed by common public law may not claim to be God's chosen people; they may not claim to be God's elected kingdom. Nor should Christ's followers attempt to take on the "form" of an earthly empire or state as the church did after Constantine. States cannot be constituted as communities of faith without doing injustice to those who hold the "wrong" faith. The people of God cannot attempt to gather together in a single, exclusive political community without doing injustice to both believers and unbelievers.

With the coming of Christ all human political authorities have been put in their proper place—under his feet. They cannot be the chief mediators between God and the earth because there is only one mediator, the Lord Jesus Christ. Every political community ought now to find its proper, humble place under Christ's *common* grace until God's kingdom is fully unveiled. Particular states should each be limited to the task of establishing public legal protection for all citizens and residents without discriminatory treatment due to differences of faith.[4]

The fact is, however, that biblical revelation has not been as influential as the Greek and Roman political traditions in shaping Western politics. The implications of biblical revelation for politics have not yet been worked out in any comprehensive detail in the West. Medieval and modern political life have been dominated more by Roman and Greek political conceptions than by biblical revelation. Modern nationalism is rooted more in the Enlightenment's revival of ancient stoicism and the new secular idealism of individual freedom than in biblical reformation.[5]

Our contemporary embarrassment about old Constantinianism, the Crusades, and Christian imperialism leads most American Christians to believe that they should not enter politics with any distinctively Christian claims because that would be to violate the supposedly neutral,

---

4. See my essays "Public Justice and True Tolerance" and "Christian Action and the Coming of God's Kingdom," in *Confessing Christ and Doing Politics*, pp. 54-62 and 88-103. See also Marshall, *Thine Is the Kingdom*; Waldron Scott, *Bring forth Justice* (Grand Rapids: Eerdmans, 1980); and John Howard Yoder, *The Politics of Jesus* (Grand Rapids: Eerdmans, 1972).

5. See Herman Dooyeweerd, *Roots of Western Culture: Pagan, Secular, and Christian Options* (Toronto: Wedge Publishing Foundation, 1979); Alan Storkey, *A Christian Social Perspective* (Leicester: Inter-Varsity Press, 1979); Marshall, *Thine Is the Kingdom*; Walter Ullmann, *A History of Political Thought: The Middle Ages* (Baltimore: Penguin Books, 1965); and Christopher Dawson, *The Gods of Revolution: An Analysis of the French Revolution* (New York: Minerva Press, 1972).

nonreligious, nondogmatic, public world of politics. This attitude reflects the power of the Enlightenment worldview and shows how far Christians themselves have departed from an integral Christian approach to all of life.[6]

On the other hand, there are many Christians in the United States today who are quite willing to call for a new engagement in politics—a recovery of older traditions they believe are more Christian than present practices. Most such Christians do not in fact call for a reestablishment of the church, but they do believe that a certain set of Christian practices, biblical laws, or traditional moralities should be imposed on the society at large to make it more Christian—especially if the majority of Americans want it.

In my opinion, both the privatizing of religion and the revival of these somewhat "imperial" designs derive from a mistaken understanding of the Bible. Leslie Newbigin expresses my conviction rather well in a brilliant little essay entitled "The Other Side of 1984." He exposes the major mistake that Christians made in accepting the Constantinian tradition, which identified "the Christian dogmatic framework with the supreme political power."[7] The church and the whole kingdom of God thereby became falsely identified with the Roman Empire. Christians should have known from God's revelation in Christ that all political authority exists by the grace of God. In the Roman imperial tradition, however, the emperor decided which religions would be approved by his "grace." When Constantine and his successors entered the office of emperor, their act of granting privilege to Christians and demoting other religions was an affront to the very heart of biblical revelation. They were asserting that Christianity would exist by the grace of the emperor and at the expense of injustice to other faiths, meaning that they would mediate God's grace to the earth. In fact, Christians should have challenged the whole imperial framework by acknowledging that governments exist by the grace of God and that no earthly kingdom can be identified as Christ's body, the church, or the kingdom of God.

The response of governing officials to the diversity of faiths on earth, as long as God gives life and breath to all creatures, should be to treat them all equitably. As Newbigin says, the West has rightly rejected the mistaken synthesis of church and state that finally broke down in the religious wars of the seventeenth century. But having now grown accustomed to the separation of church and state, most of us have not carried through with the development of a distinctively Christian, non-

---

6. See Richard John Neuhaus, *The Naked Public Square* (Grand Rapids: Eerdmans, 1984). I'll have more to say about this book at the end of this essay.

7. Newbigin, *The Other Side of 1984*, Risk Book Series (Geneva: World Council of Churches, 1983), p. 30.

Constantianian public philosophy. We have simply accepted the Enlightenment approach to politics with its nationalism and secularism. The challenge, as Newbigin presents it, is for Christians to develop a truly biblical approach to life in this world on a basis different from that of the Enlightenment.

> Christian discipleship is a following of Jesus in the power of his risen life on the way which he went. That way is neither the way of purely interior spiritual pilgrimage, nor is it the way of realpolitik for the creation of a new social order. It goes the way that Jesus went, right into the heart of the world's business and politics, with a claim which is both uncompromising and vulnerable. It looks for a world of justice and peace, not as the product of its own action but as the gift of God who raises the dead and "calls into existence the things that do not exist" (Rom. 4:17). It looks for the holy city not as the product of its policies but as the gift of God. Yet it knows that to seek escape from politics into a private spirituality would be to turn one's back on the true city. It looks for the city "whose builder and maker is God," but it knows that the road to the city goes down out of sight, the way Jesus went, into that dark valley where both our selves and all our works must disappear and be buried under the rubble of history. It therefore does not invest in any political programme . . . the hope and expectations of which belong properly only to the city which God has promised.[8]

In Jesus Christ politics has been placed in its proper light—as only *one* of our human responsibilities in this world through which we are to serve the true King. "The decision for Christians is not whether or not to become involved as Christians in public affairs. It is whether our responsibilities in the public sphere are to be discharged under the kingship of Christ or under the dominion of the evil one."[9]

In sum, my argument is on behalf of a *principled* pluralism in public life, by which I mean the recognition that the God-ordained responsibility of governing officials in modern states is to provide non-discriminatory public justice for citizens of all faiths. This is not a temporary, pragmatic accommodation to the times simply because Christians

---

8. Newbigin, *The Other Side of 1984*, pp. 36-37. See also my "From Covenant of Grace to Tolerant Public Pluralism," a paper prepared for the Workshop on Covenant and Politics at the Center for the Study of Federalism at Temple University, and soon to be published by the Center.

9. Newbigin, *The Other Side of 1984*, p. 41. See also Desmond Tutu, *Hope and Suffering* (Grand Rapids: Eerdmans, 1983); and Allan Boesak, *Black and Reformed: Apartheid, Liberation and the Calvinist Tradition* (Maryknoll, N.Y.: Orbis Books, 1984).

are too weak to gain control of government. Rather, it is an argument that democratic freedom for all citizens, a constitutional order protecting all faiths, and civil rights for every citizen grow directly, as a matter of principle, from a biblical view of the meaning of this age between the first and second comings of Christ. The "Christian" state is one that gives no special public privilege to Christian citizens but seeks justice for all as a matter of principle.

THE BIBLE, POLITICS, AND THE REALITY OF CREATION ORDER

The next line of argument that must be connected quite closely with the first concerns the structural nature of our creaturely existence.

I have argued that the *historical* context in which we live, as illumined by biblical revelation, is a context of the "between times"—the time between Christ's first and second comings. The meaning of "our time" has everything to do with *why* Christians should labor hard to build political communities that provide nondiscriminatory justice for every citizen without regard to the faith he or she holds.

But Christ's first coming in history and his promise to come again to fulfill God's promised kingdom do not constitute a "salvation history" flying above the world on a chariot of its own. Christ's first coming did not create a second world of gnostic mysteries alongside this old world. No, the Messiah, Jesus Christ, was announced as the one in and through whom all things were made in the first place (John 1:1-5; Col. 1:16-17; Heb. 1:1-3). The Redeemer King is the Lord of Creation. The meaning of human life begins at the beginning of creation, not at the moment of the incarnation. And the meaning of the beginning is not something unrelated to the Redeemer: it is what the Son of God cherished so much as his own that he came to win it back, to reconstitute it, to renew it, to make it whole and right and just once again for his Father's sake. In Christ we are restored to our rightful place as God's creatures, made in his image, to be his servants and stewards on earth.

When it comes to politics, then, we must ask not only about the "time" in which we live but also about our creaturely "identity." We must ask about the creation's order and not only about the periods of its history.

In this regard I want to argue in a biblical-creational way (in contrast to an "Aristotelian–natural law" way) that our human identity is, from the beginning, political. We were meant to be political creatures. Political life as well as everything else in creation reveals the glory of God. Government and the state were not first "given on account of sin" as an afterthought that would have had no meaning had there been no fall into sin. Political society is part of the good meaning of creation that was meant to unfold along with all other human arts and sciences and societies.[10]

A simple analogy might help to explain what I mean. Biblically speaking, family life was created by God for a positive, loving, nurturing, God-revealing purpose. Part of our identity as God's image is that we are sons and daughters and frequently mothers and fathers. The family did not arise as a technical invention to control and spank bad children. Punishment and negative discipline are not the *reason* for the family. We recognize, of course, that because of sin, parents will have to incorporate punishment into the raising of their children in order to foster healthy families. But spankings and other forms of retribution fit into a deeper, broader, and more original meaning of family life.

Life in political communities is quite different from family life, to be sure. I do not intend to describe civic life as the family writ large. Rather, the analogy is this: the *purpose* for government, the *reason* for political life is not first of all to punish wrongdoing through police officers, trial lawyers, and the military. Rather, the central meaning of political life is to be found in the positive reality of a public community— the healthy interrelationships of people through public legal means so that commerce, family life, agriculture, industry, science, art, education, and many other things can be carried on all at the same time, all in the same territory, in a harmonious and just fashion.

We recognize this reality most easily when we consider traffic laws, sewage systems, laws for business contracts, natural disaster relief, the public encouragement of education, and much more. Government exists to promote the good of public community.

Of course, due to sin, a major function of government now is to punish evildoers—to arrest the thief, to prosecute the con artist, to defend against military aggression. But the reason even for legal punishments and the occasional use of force is not simply to negate evil but to restore peace, reconcile differences, recompense the one who was wronged, recover public order, and establish justice.

Look again at the Torah and notice how God organized Israel for public justice as well as for other purposes. He did not first give commands to punish evil but rather to promote good—good health, good economic relations, ecological sanity, and so forth (Lev. 11–15; Deut. 15:1-8; 17:14-20). Look at the psalms in which prayers are lifted up to God to give the king and people justice, harmony, shalom (Pss. 45, 72, 119). Read the prophets who condemn not only the injustice of failing to

---

10. See my "Politics, Pluralism and the Ordinances of God"; Mouw, *Politics and the Biblical Drama*; and Marshall, *Thine Is the Kingdom*.

punish evil people but also the injustice of not promoting public good (Isa. 1; Jer. 22:1-17; Zech. 7).

And who, after all, is Jesus Christ, the promised Messiah? He is not simply the final judge of evil; he is the King of all kings, the ultimate Royal Monarch, who will establish justice, reconcile differences, reconstitute a healthy public life, and order the nations in justice once and for all (Isa. 9:1-7; 11; 42:1-9; Jer. 23:5-6; Matt. 28:18; Col. 1:15-20; Rev. 19:11-16). His new city will be a *real city*, ordered justly, not an informal fellowship group or a private prayer meeting or a church worship service (Rev. 21:1-27).

To describe God for us, the Bible holds up not only the shepherd, the bridegroom, the father, and the gardener but also the judge, the king, the governor, and the peacemaker. Old Israel, and the new Israel, are not collections of individuals each seeking his or her own freedom before God while having to *put up* with government as a necessary evil due to sin. No, God's people are communal creatures with responsibility for one another in all areas of life, and one of those essential areas of life is the public arena in which harmony should be promoted through just laws.

While there is no such thing as an ideal, timeless form of government or political community, political life in various historical circumstances is unavoidable. Political life is as much a part of our human identity as family life, education, eating, and drinking. The question is not whether we can or should be political but rather *how* we should practice our politics justly.

At this juncture, then, I want to enlarge the meaning of *pluralism*. Earlier I argued that the protection of a plurality of faiths is an obligation of a just government between the times of Christ's appearing. In other words, a state or political community in this age *may not* try to constitute itself as a community of one faith without doing public injustice to all faiths. As a matter of principle, therefore, I argued for what could be called "confessional pluralism."

But there is another sense in which the word *pluralism* should be used—namely, to refer to the complex social structure of the human life. We can call this "structural pluralism." God created human beings with so many different talents and characteristics and capabilities that the development of their creatureliness has brought forth all kinds of human communities, organizations, associations, institutions, and relationships. Today we take for granted the reality of farms, publishing companies, families, industries, schools, art galleries, scientific laboratories, sports teams, churches, and much more. This diverse reality is no accident of human arbitrariness. These are all expressions of our human identity in response to what God has created us to be and to do in his world. The creation's diverse law order (or "norm" order) makes for a great diversity of social structures. The term "structural pluralism" refers to this reality, and for political purposes it means that governments and public laws should recognize, protect, and do justice to this diversity.[11]

Not everything is political. Not everything should come under political control or under direction of a single authority. Human responsibilities on earth are too diverse and complex. Only God can be Lord over all. Only God in Jesus Christ can claim total authority. Within human society, all kinds of different realms of responsibility should be recognized and respected—homes, schools, enterprises, churches, and so on. Human beings must exercise all kinds of different responsibilities in response to God's ordinances for creation.

"Structural pluralism," therefore, is not merely a sophisticated way to talk about freedom or antitotalitarianism. It is first of all a reference to the reality of the creation's social structure which God intended for us to open up and unfold and develop in all its complexity. Therefore, just as we ought to be committed to confessional pluralism as a matter of principle, so we ought to be committed to structural pluralism as a matter of principle. The modern state or political community can be just only if its laws identify, respect, and protect the true diversity and complexity of human social life.

A truly just public order can be constituted as a whole only if we recognize the independent pluralistic diversity of society from the outset. The unity of any public order—whether that of a small town or that of the entire globe—can be healthy and just only if it is built as a complex whole. The very character of a just state can be realized only through constitutional and other means that acknowledge the independent identities of families, schools, businesses, churches, voluntary associations, animals, natural resources, and everything else that exists by virtue of God's creational mandate rather than by virtue of governmental fiat.[12]

A just state will be constitutionally limited in definite ways both because it is something less than God and also because it recognizes the identity of other creatures and human associations to which God has given responsibility and authority. By way of analogy, think of the sculptor who can create a beautiful statue only by doing justice to the medium

---

11. See Rockne McCarthy et al., *Society, State and Schools: A Case for Structural and Confessional Pluralism* (Grand Rapids: Eerdmans, 1981); Herman Dooyeweerd, *The Christian Idea of the State* (Nutley, N.J.: Craig Press, 1968); Storkey, *A Christian Social Perspective;* Marshall, *Thine Is the Kingdom;* and my doctoral dissertation, "The Development of Calvinistic Political Theory in the Netherlands," Duke University, 1974.

12. This argument is developed in more detail in my essay "Societal Pluralism: Blessing or Curse for the Public Good," in *The Ethical Dimension of Political Life: Essays in Honor of John H. Hallowell*, ed. Francis Canavan (Durham, N.C.: Duke University Press, 1983), pp. 166-72.

of stone or wood with which he or she begins. Or the orchestra conductor who can bring forth a harmonious symphony only by respecting the room, time, and talent of each member in the orchestra. To "sculpt" or "orchestrate" a just public order requires great insight into the particular office of responsibility that government has in a state or in an international organization. Binding a territory together under one public law will be just and good to the extent that unity is sought not by obliterating diversity, not by concentrating all authority in public offices, but by doing justice to the full diversity of institutions and authorities.

The error of Rousseau (and of numerous subsequent reformers and revolutionaries) was to want to build or regain public moral wholeness at the expense of the structural diversity of human life. Rousseau, and later Marx, was reacting to the dominating control of public life by one or more private interests. Yet Rousseau's theoretical effort to create a community governed by the general will did not make room for a genuinely complex whole. As he said in the *Social Contract*, "It is therefore of the utmost importance for obtaining the expression of the general will, that no partial society should be formed in the State, and that every citizen should speak his opinion entirely from himself." The Dutch Calvinist philosopher Herman Dooyeweerd properly criticizes Rousseau for failing to grasp the reality of social diversity and wanting to concentrate all authority in an undifferentiated public totality.[13]

Although no one of consequence in the United States today is arguing on behalf of a totalitarian society, the raging debate among liberals and conservatives usually comes down to a contest between proponents of more freedom on the one hand and proponents of more public unity or integration on the other. The liberal typically is more concerned with the relative relationship among citizens as measured by a general standard of equality. Frequently, the political liberal is willing to appeal to government to promote some good without sufficient regard for whether that action properly respects the responsibilities of other institutions, associations, and organizations. Conservatives typically criticize liberals for wanting government to interfere in too many dimensions of life, thus threatening freedom. I too am concerned with the lack of appreciation for structural pluralism in liberal and socialist political thought, and I criticize it along the lines of the argument I have been presenting here.[14]

But the majority of contemporary evangelical Christians in Amer-

---

13. Dooyeweerd, *Roots of Western Culture*, p. 170.
14. See my "Human Freedom and Social Justice: A Christian Response to the Marxist Challenge," in *The Challenge of Marxist and Neo-Marxist Ideologies for Christian Scholarship*, ed. John C. Vander Stelt (Sioux Center, Ia.: Dordt College Press, 1982), pp. 23-53.

ica are not driven by liberal tendencies. The greater pressure comes from more conservative tendencies, and I would like to relate my argument to that fact. Just as the ideal of individual freedom is inadequate as a norm for public justice, so is the desire to recover a moral America. It is simply too undifferentiated a goal to guide political action. Government should not have the authority to impose any law it wants on any arena of social life it chooses in the name of morality. Most conservative Christians think they are affirming limits on government with their call for "free enterprise" and "freedom of religion." But freedom for enterprise and religion in the West has, for the most part, been rooted in the Enlightenment's secularized notion of the autonomous individual and the private character of religion. Little if any appreciation for the character of "structural pluralism" has been exhibited in that tradition. There is nothing peculiarly Christian or biblical in a political movement that calls for the restoration of a moral America. The critical question is what would be the proper definition and constitution of a just public community, a just state, in which churches, schools, enterprises, families, the media, and the like are respected in their own right, and what part of morality would properly belong to government and public law in such a state. If this question is not answered, then a political movement for moral reconstruction is little more than the entrance of another combatant into the struggle for majoritarian control of an undifferentiated public arena. That movement can make little contribution to a biblical understanding of the differentiated identity of the state, and it may simply help to strengthen the Enlightenment tradition of secularized politics in the West.

It is even less Christian or biblical to approach politics as if it is nothing more than the arena for means-to-ends combat with others who disagree about all kinds of social ends to be achieved. In other words, to use political means to achieve various nonpolitical ends without asking what the "normative" identity and task of the state should be is to disregard the very reality of God's creation order; it is to trample carelessly over God's creation without regard to his "norms" for the character of public life. To take majoritarian, interest-group politics as now practiced in the United States for granted is to accept a political deformation that cannot provide a normative basis for achieving the ends thought to be morally imperative. Christian political responsibility requires an understanding of public justice and the kind of "just state" we are seeking. Christian politics is not a matter of picking up existing political means of whatever character and then using them to try to achieve a variety of moral (and other general) goals. Believing one knows what is morally or socially right and good is not a sufficient basis for defining a political agenda. Christians must put forward an integral public philosophy on the basis of which they can argue and contend with other citizens for the shape of a just society and a properly (normatively) limited state. They must attempt to clarify and work for a structurally differentiated community of public justice as circumscribed by the creational reality of structural pluralism and the historically timed unfolding of God's redemptive plan, which demands rigorous public protection of confessional pluralism.

POLITICS AND SIN

If politics and government are properly part of God's creational purpose for human beings, and if Christ's redemptive work includes the recovery of political vocation, then does this mean that sin is of no consequence? Does the reality of evil, of governmental oppression and the misuse of power, have no bearing on a Christian view of politics in this time between the comings of Christ? Of course not. Human sin is as great a distorting power in political life as it is in every other area of life. Apart from the grace of God in Christ which condemns disobedience and restores life, we would exist in utter darkness due to sin. Human life is depraved in all its dimensions because of sin.

At this point it might be most helpful to contrast the argument I have been making with the thinking of Reinhold Niebuhr and John Howard Yoder. Niebuhr is frequently mentioned as the preeminent twentieth-century Christian who denounced optimistic idealism and urged a return to political realism precisely because of the reality of sin. And Yoder's more recent influence in evangelical circles has come from his call for a distinctively Christian approach to social and political life based on an active confrontation with sinful political powers.

It may be true, as William Hordern has said, that Niebuhr's "most characteristic concept is that of original sin."[15] But we must recognize that Niebuhr is not unambiguous about the relationship between creation and sin. Human rebellion against God does not constitute the full explanation of political deformation and oppression in Niebuhr's view. According to Niebuhr,

> One interesting aspect of the religious yearning after the absolute is that, in the contrast between the divine and the human, all lesser contrasts between good and evil on the human and historic level are obscured. Sin finally becomes disobedience to God and nothing else. Only rebellion against God, and only the impertinence of self-will in the sight of God, are regarded as sinful. . . . The sin which the religious man feels himself committing against God is

---

15. Hordern, A *Layman's Guide to Protestant Theology*, rev. ed. (New York: Macmillan, 1968), p. 156.

indeed the sin of self-will; but his recognition of that fact may, but need not, have special social significance.[16]

What does Niebuhr mean by this? I believe that he maintained too narrow a conception of the direct relationship between God and human beings. He held that religious yearning and acts of self-will that defy God can be identified with one dimension of human life, an inner dimension of great but not universal significance. Other "lesser contrasts between good and evil" will not necessarily have any special religious character; they may have a social significance that is not directly related to God.

The significance of sin for Niebuhr, then, is not necessarily connected with the meaning of a creation that is entirely dependent on and subject to God and his ordinances. "If we contemplate the conflict between religious and political morality," he says, "it may be well to recall that the religious ideal in its purest form has nothing to do with the problem of social justice. . . . Pure religious idealism does not concern itself with the social problem."[17]

Going a step further, we can say that for Niebuhr there are no creation norms that circumscribe and make possible the structural diversity of human social life. Sin in politics does not necessarily mean the malformation of a political order that *ought* to be just as defined by divine law. Rather, for Niebuhr, *social* sin is the inevitable distortion of life that comes from the very nature of human finitude and weakness in this world. Social sin is a natural necessity, unavoidable as long as we are human, but it cannot be defined or exposed by a creational norm that shows what it is a distortion of. According to Niebuhr, "Any kind of significant social power develops social inequality."[18]

Political action, therefore, cannot be carried out with the conviction that we can attempt to foster a just state by recognizing and obeying certain divine norms that govern the creation. Social sin, in contrast to disobedience toward God, is, for Niebuhr, an ever-present, built-in ambiguity in the very nature of social activity. God's judgment and redemption of the world through Christ are not sufficient to enlighten the path on which we now walk as Christians in the political world. Sin and ambiguity are somehow built into our human condition.

Certainly anyone who enters actively into politics should work for the best answers to problems, says Niebuhr. But this will be little more than choosing the lesser of two evils, and, in democratic countries, trying to find "proximate solutions for insoluble problems." To whatever de-

---

16. Niebuhr, *Moral Man and Immoral Society* (New York: Scribner's, 1960), p. 67.
17. Niebuhr, *Moral Man and Immoral Society, p.* 263.
18. Niebuhr, *Moral Man and Immoral Society, pp.* 7-8.

gree this sounds realistic, it faces at least the problem that John Hallowell points out—namely, that since Niebuhr rejects "any conception of absolute and universal justice, it is difficult to understand what the solutions are to 'approximate' or how we are to determine or evaluate the degree of 'proximity' attained."[19]

Niebuhr's realism looks more like a fatalism or resignation in the face of ambiguity. Ambiguity itself becomes a norm or guide for action. In my judgment, Niebuhr was not realistic enough about the universality of sin as disobedience to God; nor was he sufficiently open to the power of God's judging and redeeming work in Christ, through whom sin is exposed and the truth brought to light.

As for John Howard Yoder, he indicates his understanding of the relation between creation order and sinful disobedience in his exposition of Colossians 1:15-17 and Romans 12–13. There is no doubt, he says, that all powers were created in, through, and for Christ. They are manifestations of the "reign of order among creatures, order which in its original intention is a divine gift."[20] They were originally part of God's good creation.

The problem, however, is that human beings have fallen into sin and no longer have "access to the good creation of God." The fall is not total in the sense that the "powers" have not become "limitlessly evil"— "the Powers, despite their fallenness, continue to exercise an ordering function." But the situation is ambiguous in that the original creation order is somehow closed off while at the same time sin has not totally distorted the creation. The fallen powers are "necessary to life and society, but . . . have claimed the status of idols and have succeeded in making men serve them as if they were of absolute value."[21]

In these few brief statements Yoder has expressed a conception of sin and creation as ambiguous as Niebuhr's. In both cases, I would argue, the error comes in not distinguishing actual, sinfully distorted, human institutions from the good creation order. It is not God's law, God's normative ordinances, the creation order that is ambiguous or has fallen into sin. That order is precisely what stands over against actualized human institutions, exposing them as relatively unjust or just as the case may be. Human beings and their social formations are sinful and disobedient to divine ordinances; it is not God's good creation ordinances that have been deformed.

The other side of this is that the *fallen* powers are not what gives order to society; they are precisely what brings disorder. The fallen

---

19. Hallowell, *Main Currents in Modern Political Thought* (New York: Holt, Rinehart & Winston, 1950), p. 671.

20. Yoder, *The Politics of Jesus*, p. 143.

21. Yoder, *The Politics of Jesus*, p. 144.

powers are not necessary to life; they are what leads to death. Order in the creation is maintained by God's gracious upholding of the creation's good order *despite* (and in confrontation with) the sinful powers, not by means of them. Indeed, I would argue, by God's redeeming grace we *do* have access to the good creation, for if we did not, there would be no way to recognize either sin or restoration for what they are. [22]

Having failed to distinguish the normativity of the good creation from the positivized sinfulness of human actions, Yoder is driven to posit an ambiguity in the meaning of Christ's redemption not unlike the ambiguity in Niebuhr. Since our subordination to "fallen powers" is what makes us human, according to Yoder, then if "God is going to save man *in his humanity*, the Powers cannot simply be destroyed or set aside or ignored. Their sovereignty must be broken." [23] But surely Yoder does not mean that it is the good creation that Christ had to break; it is only man's sinful distortion that had to be broken. And the breaking of sin brings a real restoration of creation in accord with the original character and order given it by God.

The ambiguity in which Yoder is caught comes to especially clear focus when he discusses Romans 13. There he assumes that the exercise of "wrathful violence" (13:4) is, by definition, the opposite of Christian love. Governments by their nature must exercise violence and killing that can in no way be made a "channel of the will of God." [24] A little later, however, Yoder contends that there is a norm for government whereby we can judge whether God's will is being accomplished by the governmental minister. Romans 13 teaches us that the ministers of God are ministers *"only to the extent to which* they carry out their function. . . . We can judge and measure the extent to which a government is accomplishing its ministry, by asking namely whether it persistently [*present* participle] attends to the rewarding of good and evil according to their merits; to be 'minister to you for good' is a criterion, not a description." He goes on to say, "We are instructed to give government certain types of 'honor' or 'fear.' The place of government in the providential designs of God is not such that our duty would be simply to do whatever it says." [25]

Clearly, then, Yoder holds that God has ordained a responsibility for government to fulfill in accord with a certain normative obligation. We are subject as Christians not to any government doing anything it

22. The same dialectic between sin and grace without a strong doctrine of creation can be found in Jim Wallis's *Agenda for Biblical People* (New York: Harper & Row, 1976).

23. Yoder, *The Politics of Jesus*, p. 147.

24. Yoder, *The Politics of Jesus*, p. 204.

25. Yoder, *The Politics of Jesus*, p. 211.

wants, but to government performing its God-ordained task. Thus, we are *not* subject to fallen powers on their own terms, in their sinful condition. We are not enjoined to obey evil commands of those powers. Rather, we are subject to the Lord in all things and are subject to government by God's command in order to fulfill his justice. Likewise, governments are also subject to the norm Yoder has enunciated, and insofar as they do not serve the Lord in rendering justice, they are not his obedient servants.

That insight, it seems to me, should have driven Yoder back to a reexamination of his conviction that the use of the sword as such is always a violation of Christian love to God and neighbor. Instead of insisting on the disjunction between Romans 12:9 and 13:4 as he does, Yoder ought to have seen that God's establishment of the earthly office of government for the exercise of God's wrath against the evildoer is *God's* act and *God's* command. Precisely because Christians must leave vengeance and wrath to the Lord, they should not be unwilling to exercise an office that God himself has established for the accomplishment of that task. Nor is there any reason to assume that God's authority over all things in Christ is not to be obeyed by Christians in all areas of life as a consistent expression of their love for God and neighbor. Why not assume that God's normative task for government (Rom. 13) is consistent with the responsibilities that he lays on Christians in all areas of life "inside the perfection of Christ"?

The unique character of government, I would contend, is that it is normed by God to do justice. Killing, murder, and *human* vengeance are no more a legitimate part of that office than they are a legitimate part of an individual's office of loving servanthood. Earthly governments are commissioned to use the sword only in a way that is fully in accord with God's will. A man who fills the office of earthly governor does so legitimately only as a servant of God for good—namely, to punish the evil person and to reward the good person. That task in no way includes the command to try to bring in Christ's kingdom by force. It in no way allows the earthly governor to do something that is not in conformity with God's rule over the whole earth in Christ. The governmental officeholder is a servant of the Lord, not a human overlord in his or her own right. Earthly government is normed as a ministry for justice and mercy, and it accomplishes its task when, for example, it protects people from the violent injustices they are prone to commit against one another.

Surely the ministry of public justice, normed by God's creational and redemptive ordinances, is an office for Christian service in fulfillment of the love command which Christ has given us. Yoder's hermeneutical disjunction between Romans 12 and 13 seems difficult to maintain. Any distortion of that office or misuse of the sword in that office cannot be attributed to some nonevangelical command from God or to a creation order from which Christians should be separated in their obedience to the gospel. Rather, the misuse of force by government must be judged as sin and accounted for as such in terms of the good order of creation in Christ by which he brings all sin into judgment. The Christian's call to loving service in Christ is to reform and renew even the office of earthly government in accord with the norms of a redeemed creation.

AMERICAN DEMOCRACY AND BIBLICAL OBEDIENCE TO JUSTICE

Against the backdrop of the general discussion above, I would like to enter a discussion of American politics by focusing attention on two important issues—one having to do with the First Amendment to the Constitution, the other having to do with the shape of the American electoral system. In both cases, the purpose will be to demonstrate how a commitment to confessional and structural pluralism provides a distinctive approach to American government and politics. We will turn, first of all, to the contemporary First Amendment concern with education as that raises questions about the role of the state in relation to faith, family life, and schools.

In 1925, in a case called *Pierce v. Society of Sisters* (268 U.S. 510 1925), the U.S. Supreme Court upheld the right of parents to choose schools for their children other than those established by the state of Oregon.[26] And yet the Court did not fully establish the right of parents to be *principally* responsible for th education of their children: it did not go so far as to invalidate the dominant tradition of state "principalship" in education. At best the decision was a recognition that parental authority in education cannot be discarded altogether. At worst it seemed to seal forever the second-class and subordinate status of parents in the realm of education. The state has first right to establish the institutional framework for education; parents have the subordinate right to opt out of that state-established framework if they can afford to do so.

That judgment by the Court (and all school decisions since 1925) was justified by the argument that the parent's choice of a nongovernment school is a private, usually religious choice that cannot be supported by equitable public recognition and funding without entangling government in the establishment of religion.

To resolve various problems and disputes connected with government and education it will be necessary, I believe, to change our assumptions about *principalship* and *agency* in education within the framework of what I've described as "structural" pluralism. This cannot be done,

---

26. For more on this, see Stephen Arons, "The Separation of School and State: *Pierce* Reconsidered," *Harvard Educational Review* 46 (1976): 76ff.

however, without giving serious attention to the importance of government's responsibility for justice and equity in society. The ongoing ambiguity and contradiction in American education policy will never be satisfactorily resolved until we recognize *both* that government has a legitimate and proper concern for the well-being of citizens (including their educational well-being) and that government cannot do justice to everyone involved in education until it recognizes in law the independent reality of families and schools and establishes that parents hold the full obligation of *principalship* for their minor children. The change in assumptions at this point leads, necessarily, to changes in assumptions about the meaning of "public vs. private" and "sacred vs. secular."

In the first place, the family should be recognized in its own right as something that is neither an individual person nor a department of state. Government should neither swallow up family members by treating them simply as citizens, thus abrogating their rights and identities as family members, nor accept the total isolation and autonomy of all the individuals involved as if their individuality gives them some right to absolute privacy and public unaccountability.[27]

Second, we should change the focus of our attention when it comes to educational agencies—the schools. A school is an agency for education. It is built on a philosophy of education; it hires teachers who have different ideas about how to train students in different disciplines; it must stand *in loco parentis* and thereby deal amicably and in a trustworthy fashion with parents; it takes in *students* who thereby have a role in school distinguishable from the role of *family member* in a family and *citizen* in the civil community. In other words, schools are schools and not simply extensions of families or the government. They have a life of their own with a peculiar identity and quality to them. Government ought to acknowledge the actual and diverse reality of schools just as it should the reality of families. Government does not deal with individual citizens-in-general; it deals with citizens who are at the same time family members and school participants, among many other things.

The rightful recognition of schools as schools would not require the government to relinquish all concern for education. It would not even imply that the government should close down all of its own "agencies" of education. The consequences, rather, would be that government would look upon schools, including its own, as distinct agencies of education rather than as mere departments of state.

---

27. On rights of families and other institutions and associations, see McCarthy et al., *Society, State, and Schools*, pp. 63-78; cf. Bruce C. Hafen, "The Constitutional Status of Marriage, Kinship, and Sexual Privacy: Balancing the Individual and Social Interests," *Michigan Law Review* 81 (January 1983): 570ff.

Third, government's identity and responsibility should be reconsidered. Government *does* have responsibility to secure public justice, including justice in education, for all its citizens. But the government's approach to education ought to be within the public legal framework that *takes for granted both the principalship of parents in the education of their children and the right of schools to be schools in offering their services for the education of these children.*

The first major consequences of this shift in assumptions will be to open up genuine *parental choice* of schooling for children.[28] At present parents can only choose between using the district public school or opting out of that system at their own expense. This simply is not a choice for many with low incomes, and it is an unfair choice even for those with sufficient income. If parents are truly the principals in the education of their children, then government should treat the educational choices of all parents equitably.

Moreover, parents will not really be able to choose from among different educational agencies until public law removes the unjust privileges it gives to its own school agencies. In other words, coincident with recognizing parents as the principals in the education of their children there must come the recognition of those agencies which parents choose. Every school must have the same legal and financial opportunity to open its doors to the public to offer its services.

At this juncture let us bring in the question of religion. What if some parents select a school that happens to be run by the Catholic Church? If the government supports such a school, whether directly or indirectly, does it become illegitimately entangled in religion or run the danger of establishing a religion? To the contrary, failure to allow parental choice of "religious" schools would constitute discrimination against some religions as well as against some parents. The only establishment danger would rise if the government decided to give special benefit to those who attend Catholic schools over against those who attend Presbyterian or public schools. A fair and equitable distribution of funds for the purpose of education as argued here would establish nothing but the value of education in the context of parental choice and freedom for all schools.

With this approach, the dispute over "religion" versus "secularity" is removed from the arena of education. Religion is not simply what goes on in churches and in some individual consciences; it is also the way many people choose to live, including the way they choose to raise and educate their children. Government should not have the constitutional

---

28. On this, see the new journal *Equity and Choice*, published by the Institute for Responsive Education, Boston; see also Joe Nathan, *Free to Teach* (Minneapolis: Winston Press, 1984).

right to predefine the limits and scope of religion. Nor should it have the concomitant right to give itself a monopoly over the so-called "secular" world. What government must do is give full attention to the welfare of the entire public and always mandate, through law, what is in the public interest. If its mandates happen to include the mandate of education for every citizen, then government must see to it that the mandate is carried out in a way that does justice to the full diversity of children, parents, teachers, schools, and other people and organizations involved in education. If some citizens choose to make education part of their religious practice while others prefer to identify schooling with something they consider irreligious or nonreligious, then so be it. That is not government's responsibility.

Now, in the second place, let me direct attention toward our American electoral system in order to demonstrate how a commitment to confessional and structural pluralism might express itself there. Earlier I criticized some of today's conservative Christians for simply taking for granted the legitimacy of majoritarian, interest-group politics as the means by which they ought to fight for moral renewal or reconstruction. That is a mistake not only because politics should concern itself with a specifically *public* morality but also because the means themselves should be just.

The following argument draws from a proposal put forward by the Association for Public Justice several years ago to revitalize and make more just the democratic processes of American politics.[29] Our concern is not simply with certain policy outcomes but with the shape of the political and electoral systems themselves. We support democratic political institutions as an *essential* part of the composition of a contemporary, differentiated state. Therefore, we are critical of those features of our system that do not adequately represent the diversity of communities and people in this country. This proposal seeks to address that problem.

For purposes of illustration, let me focus on the U.S. House of Representatives, for which redistricting occurs on a regular ten-year schedule. What should now be enlarged, we argue, are the criteria for judging the meaning of redistricting for House elections. Mere quantitative measurement of numbers is not enough. How the diversity of viewpoints among citizens is represented should be considered crucial in judging the quality of an electoral system. A step in the right direction would be made if each state would redistrict itself into a *single district*. Each state would still be eligible to send a certain number of representatives to the House (its proportional percentage of the 435) based on the

---

29. For more on this, see the Association for Public Justice position paper "Toward Just Representation."

size of its population. But it would select those representatives by means of *proportional representation* within that single district rather than by means of an equivalent number of separate, winner-take-all districts.

Very simply, the system would work like this. Any number of parties could put forward as many candidates as that state is eligible to send to the House in Washington. For example, let's take a state that currently has twenty representatives in the House. Any number of parties could put forward 20 statewide candidates. Voters would vote for the candidates of their choice with the seats being allocated on the basis of the proportion of votes that each party receives. If the Republicans, for example, win 60 percent of the statewide vote, they would get 60 percent of the House seats (12 out of 20). If a new "Popular People's Party" wins 10 percent of the vote, it would get 2 seats. If the Democrats win 30 percent of the votes, they would get 6 seats. In our present system it would be very likely that a party with only 10 percent of the votes would never gain representation. It is also likely that the Republicans would win more than 12 out of 20 seats if their largest opposition party could muster only 30 percent of the votes.

Not only would a proportional system make it possible for smaller parties to emerge in many states, but it would also make possible the strengthening of the party system as a whole. Since the aim of an election would no longer have to be simply winning the majority vote, each party would be free to present and stand for its own principles and programs without losing the likelihood of having a voice in Congress. In fact, one could say that parties would be forced to clarify and distinguish themselves from one another rather than doing the opposite as is now usually the case.

The purpose of this brief argument on behalf of proportional representation is to illustrate the importance of the electoral system in a democratic country. Electoral systems vary widely and function differently depending on their rules and structures. Those who believe in a limited state that ought to be securing justice for the confessional and structural diversity in society should carry forward their concern into the very institutions of government and politics. Some degree of proportional representation in American politics would enhance the quality of democratic representation. It would also help to reinforce other features of proportional pluralism, as illustrated by my argument for educational pluralism. This is, I believe, a consistent if not necessary expression of a biblically rooted approach to political responsibility as developed in the first sections of this paper.

There are, of course, other dimensions to public justice than just the principle of proportionality. Proportional justice cannot solve all problems or guide the formulation of all public policies. Yet the argument for proportional justice in education and representation illustrates the way I would contend for the expression of Christian political responsibility in these areas of concern.

THE NECESSITY OF AN INTEGRAL APPROACH TO POLITICAL RESPONSIBILITY

In conclusion, I would like to draw together various strands of the arguments I have presented in order to make the case that politics, from a biblical point of view, requires serious, integral, organized attention from Christian citizens. In other words, those who reject a sacred/secular dualism (as I do), who see the meaning of creation and redemption as an integral revelation of God in Christ, and who see politics as an integral part of a judged and redeemed creation will come to the conclusion that politics cannot be sidestepped or taken lightly or merely used as a means or dismissed as demonic. Political life ought to be taken up by Christians with as much seriousness as they take up their family lives, their business lives, and their church lives. And the nature of modern politics and government, I believe, requires serious, organized action.

Partly because he is hosting this conference, but more importantly because his book *The Naked Public Square: Religion and Democracy in America* is so valuable, I would like to argue with Richard John Neuhaus in the concluding pages of this paper in order to make my case for the need of an integral Christian approach to political life and thought.

The *Naked Public Square* is a provocative book that probes deeply into American politics and religion but does not clarify sufficiently the *political* nature of the problems it uncovers. The main question for Neuhaus concerns the quality of religion and culture in America. Even though the title of his book includes the words "public square" and "democracy," Neuhaus does not give a great deal of attention to the peculiar identity and structure of politics and government. Consequently, he fails to analyze or criticize the most important *political* challenges coming from secularism—namely, the idea of a nonreligious politics as well as the actual public legal discrimination against certain kinds of religious practice.

Unfortunately, Neuhaus seems to take for granted a rather "low" view of politics as a functional, means-to-end power struggle. For example, he writes that

> Politics is the business (more art than science) of governing. It has to do most essentially with power—getting, keeping, and exercising it. I am aware that this is not a very elevated view of politics. Politics can involve nobler works and even visions. But they are not essentially what politics is about. We should resist being taken in by

inflated and romantic views of politics. . . . In the most fetching evasion of this reality [the reality of politics as power], the rulers insist upon being called public servants. . . .

Attention must be paid the political, then, not because politics bestows meaning upon our lives but because, if we do not, others will pay attention. . . . Biblical people should not be surprised by this view of government. We have been instructed to have no illusions about the principalities and powers short of the kingdom of God. At the deepest level, our feeling of alienation is not disease but sign of health. [30]

In these quotations one gets from Neuhaus the impression that politics is neither essentially human nor central to the divine call to human service. "Public servant" is apparently a term to which arrogant or naive rulers lay an illegitimate claim. Democracy is simply a practical way of limiting the power struggles of the people. Attention has to be paid to politics to keep it in its place rather than because it is an arena of high human achievement and fulfillment normed by divine standards of justice. The religious and moral reality of life is somehow outside of politics and enters politics through the moral persons who have to "pay attention" to politics. The political world is under Christ's lordship not as a domain of his glorious revelation but as a temporary means of control until the real kingdom comes.

By contrast, when Neuhaus turns late in his book to a discussion of *law*, he does so with little reference to politics. Clearly his view of politics as something connected with a compromising power struggle is almost disconnected from his conception of law, which he wants to associate with transcendent meaning. Consider the following:

Law speaks of what is authoritative in a society.

Laws may be just or unjust, wise or foolish, but behind the laws is the law.

Laws issue from and participate in "the law." The law is more than a body of rules; it is the historical, living process of people legislating, adjudicating, administering, and negotiating the allocation of rights and duties. Its purpose is to prevent harm, resolve conflicts, and create means of cooperation. Its premise, from which it derives its perceived legitimacy and therefore its authority, is that it strives to anticipate and give expression to what a people believes to be its collective destiny or ultimate meaning within a moral universe. [31]

---

30. Neuhaus, *The Naked Public Square: Religion and Democracy in America* (Grand Rapids: Eerdmans, 1984), pp. 30-31.

31. Neuhaus, *The Naked Public Square*, pp. 248, 250, 253.

What Neuhaus fails to see, in my judgment, is that the state—the political community of rulers and subjects—is an integral order of *public laws* based on the *right and power of enforcement*. Instead, he connects the "power" and "force" of the state with *low* politics while connecting "laws" and "legality" with *high* moral purpose and transcendent sources. Politics and power must be kept limited, held back from totalitarian tendencies, viewed as outside the essential meaning of human life. Law and its moral source, on the other hand, are elevated to a place of authority and transcendence central to human meaning. But this split will not work. There is no power politics apart from the struggle to define and implement public laws. There are no public laws apart from the political, constitutional, juridical processes. What I have called God's creational law order, or norm order (and what Neuhaus wants to call "*the* law") should not be associated with "laws" over against "power." Rather, God's normative law order should be seen as "holding for" every human institution and association in its factual wholeness, each in its own sphere. Neuhaus misses the integral identity of the state or political community as an institution of *both* law and power (and much, much more). Neither law nor power can be abstracted from the publicly governed community.

If we are to have a revitalized America with a significant contribution from Christians to the shape of public life, then we need an integral and organized effort in politics. Individual votes and letters along with commentary and criticism from individuals will not be enough. Political change requires organized action rooted in a solid public philosophy.

My arguments in this paper have been in support of a particular view of political life—a view of citizens under government working for communities of public justice as part of their creaturely calling in God's redeemed creation. If states should be communities of public justice as ordained by God's creational ordinances, then Christians should accept God's judgment of sin and his redemption of the creation through Christ as his call to them to renew, among other things, their political responsibilities in obedience to him. American democracy must be "taken on" by a direct challenge to its unjust deformities and by a conserving concern for its healthy embodiments of justice. But this reformation and conservation can be pursued only by highly energized and organized political efforts rooted in a solidly biblical view of the state. Without ongoing, day-by-day associational action among citizens who share a burden of concern for the justice of their country and their world, the debate over a Christian view of politics will remain academic.

Evangelicalism and Survey Research: Interpretative Problems and Substantive Findings

Corwin Smidt and Lyman Kellstedt

Over the past decade, American scholars have shown a renewed interest in the role that religion plays within American politics. While a variety of factors have contributed to this renewed interest, both the apparent growth and the increased political militancy evident among American evangelical Christians have helped to spark the renewed attention. Among those political scientists who are engaged in the study of electoral behavior, these changes have prompted a reexamination of whether religion constitutes a "primary" or a "secondary" variable in explaining American electoral behavior generally and have also prompted a new focus on the political nature and electoral importance of American evangelical Christians in particular.

However, while there has been increased scholarly attention given to the evangelical community, major problems confront any analyst who attempts to study the topic. These problems are of such proportions that they will significantly affect both the nature of the findings and the analysis made in this study. Consequently, it is first necessary to review briefly these specific problems in order to assist the reader in evaluating the form, substance, and "validity" of the material we present here.

ANALYTICAL PROBLEMS

The Data Problem. The first problem confronting any analyst is the lack of national surveys specifically designed to analyze the political attitudes and behavior of the evangelical community. Most national surveys prior to 1980 included few religious questions beyond denominational affiliation and church attendance. Religion was considered to be a "secondary" rather than a "primary" variable—that is, it was assumed that much of the "effect" of religion could be attributed to variation in the socioeconomic status among individuals. Moreover, whatever remaining variance that could possibly be attributed to religious variables generally was assumed to represent some dying vestige of influence from the past, as the process of secularization increasingly diminished the scope and influence of the religious sphere of life.

However, changes during the 1970s challenged this perspective, and scholars began to reexamine the role of religion in contemporary life. As a result, social and political researchers began to incorporate new questions in their surveys that were designed to tap various religious attitudes and characteristics of the respondents.

Unfortunately, these additional questions have been few in number and unsystematic in their focus. For example, some surveys have added a question pertaining to whether the respondent has had a "born again" experience (e.g., the *New York Times*/CBS exit poll), others have added questions tapping the respondent's view of the Bible and images of God (e.g., the General Social Surveys of the National Opinion Research Center), while still others have added several questions tapping the importance of religion, "born again" experiences, and views of the Bible (e.g., the national election studies of the University of Michigan's Center for Political Studies). Thus, overall, such studies have remained relatively "rich" in the number and variety of the political and social questions they ask but relatively "poor" in the number, variety, and quality of the religious questions they ask. On the other hand, there have been some surveys that have incorporated a large number of religious questions, enabling the researcher to identify with greater confidence which respondents might be classified as evangelicals (e.g., the *Christianity Today* poll and the Unchurched American survey), but these have tended to include relatively few political and social questions. And, finally, there have been at least some recent surveys that appear to have a good mix of religious and political questions (e.g., several Gallup polls conducted through the Princeton Religion Research Center), but these have not been readily, if at all, available to scholars.

Consequently, any scholar who wishes to analyze the political attitudes and behavior of American evangelicals in a systematic manner finds that there is little adequate data to work with. Because few religious questions tend to be asked in most social surveys, any such analysis at this time will of necessity be relatively simple in terms of its operational measure of evangelicalism. And because such surveys vary in the religious and political questions they ask, any such analysis will of necessity be largely composed of fragmented pieces of evidence taken from various surveys, and findings based on such data must be viewed as suggestive rather than conclusive.

The Conceptual Problems. Even if data problems can be surmounted, various conceptual problems remain. There is a lack of scholarly agreement as to the nature of the evangelical movement and to the parameters within which evangelicals are to be defined. There are several distinct ways in which evangelicalism, despite its internal diversity, can be viewed as a single phenomenon. [1] One approach is to use the term "evangelical" to refer to some specific *conceptual* entity abstractly identified and unified by the analyst. This approach may emphasize subscription to certain theological beliefs (e.g., beliefs concerning the nature of Jesus Christ and scriptural authority), some manifestation of certain religious characteristics (e.g., having had a "born again" experience or attending church on some regular basis), or a combination of the two.

Various analytical issues are associated with this first approach. For example, just how broadly or how narrowly should the term "evangelical" be used in reference to orthodox Christianity? While evangelicals adhere to the orthodox tenets of the Christian faith, does subscription to such tenets alone, however formulated, qualify one as an evangelical? Or are there unique characteristics that tend to differentiate evangelicals from other orthodox Christians? For example, in most of the work done by Gallup, only those reporting a "born again" experience are classified as evangelicals. [2] On the other hand, James Hunter differentiates between confessional and conversional evangelicals and does not insist upon a "born again" experience as an absolute prerequisite for being classified as an evangelical. [3]

Moreover, if the emphasis is merely upon subscription to certain theological beliefs, then less attention tends to be placed upon the historical context in which such beliefs originated and the social context within which they are expressed. Thus, all those who subscribe to the designated beliefs tend to be classified as evangelicals—regardless, for example, of whether they are Protestant or Catholic, white or black. To view evangelicals as a conceptual unity places greater emphasis upon atomistic conceptions of how evangelicals relate to the world around them. Those who work from such a perspective may attempt to ascertain the effect that certain religious beliefs, experiences, or practices may have upon politi-

---

1. On this, see George Marsden's introduction to *Evangelicalism and Modern America*, ed. George Marsden (Grand Rapids: Eerdmans, 1984), pp. ix-xvi.

2. See, for example, Gallup, "Divining the Devout: The Polls and Religious Belief," *Public Opinion* 4 (April-May 1981): 20.

3. See Hunter, *American Evangelicalism* (New Brunswick, N.J.: Rutgers University Press, 1983).

cal attitudes and behavior. As such, they tend to downplay the social context in which such beliefs, experiences, or practices may occur.

The second approach is to view evangelicalism less as an abstract category and more as a *social* reality—as a "dynamic movement, with common heritages, common tendencies, an identity, and an organic character."[4] Different subgroups within contemporary evangelicalism may be somewhat diverse and disconnected, and yet these subgroups may have the same roots and substantial historical experiences in common. The common roots can, as Marsden notes, result in commonalities (e.g., views of the Bible, styles of prayer, techniques of evangelism, behavior mores)—despite diversity in many religious particulars among the subgroups. It is the presence of such commonalities plus the sharing of substantial historical experiences that can contribute to the formation of a common identity that transcends specific differences in heritages and emphases. Consequently, it is the presence of such commonalities and, for many, the recognition of a common identity that allows the analyst to view evangelicalism as a larger social movement and as a distinct socio-religious group.

To view evangelicals as an organic unity, however, is to place at least some emphasis on the fact that religious beliefs, experiences, and practices tend to be expressed within a larger subculture. This subculture may be largely influenced by these religious expressions, but it is never totally formed by such expressions: religious groups can never be totally isolated from the larger society in which they are found. And, because the religious beliefs, experiences, and practices of evangelicals are expressed within a subcultural context, their political attitudes and behavior ought not to be considered to derive solely from those specific religious beliefs, experiences, or practices. While the expression of similar religious beliefs, the profession of similar religious experiences, and the manifestation of similar religious behavior may contribute to a convergence in the political characteristics of white and black evangelicals, the subcultural context in which these religious expressions transpire may be of greater influence than the commonalities they share; black and white evangelicals may well act differently with regard to politics despite sharing similar religious beliefs and displaying similar religious behavior.

The Measurement Problems. Finally, there are major measurement problems that confront any person who seeks to analyze survey data in order to ascertain the political attitudes, values, and behavior of evangelicals. Survey researchers are well aware that, under certain circumstances, question wording has an important impact on the responses they

---

4. Marsden, *Evangelicalism and Modern America*, p. x.

receive. Even slight variations in the wording of particular questions can markedly affect the nature of one's findings. Thus, in analyzing the characteristics of evangelicals across different national surveys, it is advantageous to employ similar questions, phrased identically, in defining evangelicals. Unfortunately, however, such surveys have not utilized similar questions, and so those who are classified as evangelicals across the different surveys may not be totally identical in nature (though there may be considerable overlap across those respondents who are identified as evangelicals).

For example, one of the most commonly used measures of evangelicalism is a "born again" question. The question posed to tap this phenomenon varies from survey to survey, and so they report different percentages of the population who admit to being "born again." Such differences are evident in Table 1 (see pp. 131-59 for the Tables mentioned herein), which presents the variation in the "born again" question found within different surveys and the resulting variation in the percentage of respondents who were classified as having had a "born again" experience.

Data analysts are also aware that measurement error is present with any operational measure of a theoretical concept. Thus, variation may result not only from differences in the question format but also from differences in measurement error associated with different operational indicators. Experiences are highly subjective in nature, and the social meaning of having had a "born again" experience, for example, may be somewhat different from its meaning within a specifically Christian context. Thus, to use a "born again" question without additional criteria can easily result in measurement error if one is attempting to identify evangelicals.

Table 2 attempts to demonstrate this problem. It presents the results from a national study done by the Gallup organization in 1978 entitled "The Unchurched American." Within this particular study, a total of 686 respondents, or 32.6 percent of the sample, said that they were "born again." Yet, as shown in Table 2, 92 of the 686 "born again" respondents stated that they had not made a commitment to Jesus Christ and 118 of the 686 respondents stated that they were not "certain" that Jesus rose from the dead.

Nevertheless, careful analysis can help to reduce such measurement error. Obviously, on conceptual grounds one might argue that those respondents who report having had a "born again" experience but who never have committed themselves to Christ, who have a "low" view of Scripture, who never pray, who lack certainty about the resurrection, and who do not think of Christ as more than human just do not belong in the evangelical category. When these are removed, the number of "born again" Christians in the Unchurched American study drops from 686

(32.6 percent) to 452 (21.5 percent), a substantial drop. Is such a procedure justified? Table 3 compares those "born again" respondents with "suspect credentials" with the other "born again" respondents. The data are clear: the "suspect" respondents differ dramatically from the other "born again" respondents and most closely resemble those who report not having had a "born again" experience. This analysis illustrates the problems that can develop when appropriate precautions are not followed in using the "born again" question as a simple operational measure for identifying evangelicals.

Yet, the analysis also reveals that there are often ways to avoid such problems. It is important that future research efforts pay careful attention to these measurement problems. Researchers should be alert to the nuances of question wording and examine questions used in prior surveys before going into the field. They should also run checks on the indicators before accepting responses as valid measures of the concepts, along the lines indicated in Tables 2 and 3. (For a similar example, but pertaining to the respondents' views of Scripture, see Appendix A, p. 160).

Finally, analysts should be sensitive to differences in the sampling variances evident within different surveys they employ. All major national surveys seek to draw representative samples, but, while random procedures are used, cluster sampling is generally employed because true random sampling is not economically feasible. In addition, different types of samples can be drawn. For example, Stuart Rothenberg and Frank Newport attempted to draw a random sample of 1,000 registered evangelical voters in their analysis of the evangelical voter,[5] but since registered voters tend to be better educated than those who are not registered to vote, their resulting sample of evangelicals tends to be more highly educated than evangelicals are as a whole (see Table 4). There may be age, regional, racial, educational, and gender differences from one survey to the next, and the different distributions of these characteristics within each survey can influence the nature of the bivariate relationships that emerge within each survey.

OUR STUDY

Having noted the limitations of available data and the precautions necessary in interpreting such data, pragmatic considerations prompt us to move on to a review of the findings that emerge from the available data. We used different data sets in part because different surveys asked differ-

---

5. See Rothenberg and Newport, *The Evangelical Voter* (Washington, D.C.: Free Congress, 1984).

ent political questions and because it permitted us to do analysis of change over time.

Because of the variation in questions from one survey to the next, we had to use different operational measures of evangelicalism. The different surveys used different numbers and different kinds of questions to identify evangelicals. In some surveys, evangelicals tend to be defined as "conversional" (i.e., having had conversion experiences), while in other studies, in which additional questions were asked, attempts were also made to identify those who might be classified as "confessional" (or non–"born again") evangelicals. The specific operational definitions associated with the various surveys are presented in Table 5. (For a brief discussion of our thinking concerning the analysis of evangelicalism by means of secondary analysis of data, see Appendix B, p. 162.)

It should also be noted that we have tended to limit our examination of evangelicals in this study to whites. Because of subcultural differences, white evangelicals differ from black evangelicals. While it would have been interesting to make comparisons and contrasts between the political attitudes and behavior of black and white evangelicals, the surveys we used contain so small an amount of data on black evangelicals that our results would necessarily have been highly uncertain.

Finally, one other note of caution must be made. Because the anti-Semitism study of 1981 oversamples Jews, analysis must be limited to white Protestants and Catholics whenever comparisons are made in which the 1981 survey is employed. Therefore, in some tables the data base is composed of white Protestant and Catholic respondents, whereas in other tables it is composed simply of white respondents. The specific data base is noted at the top of each table. Where no specification is given, the data base is composed of all respondents—regardless of race or religion.

Size and Composition. Evangelicals constitute a major segment of the American electorate and hence, at least potentially, an important bloc of voters. As can be seen from Table 6, the percentage of evangelicals varies considerably depending on what operational measures were employed and whether Catholics and/or blacks are included. Note that in Table 6, the operational measure of evangelicalism does not include the "born again" item except for the Michigan voting studies of 1980 and 1984. It is important to recognize that the diversity of measures makes comparisons difficult. Clearly, there is a great need for ongoing surveys to be aware of the measures used by others. Note also that the major surveys conducted by the National Opinion Research Center are omitted altogether because they contain no Christological measures whatsoever. Of the studies included, the *Christianity Today* (hereafter *CT*) survey has the broadest set of measures, while the Michigan voting studies and the Connecticut Mutual effort have the most narrow. The

Unchurched American survey includes a fair number of evangelical measures, but they are not "demanding measures" (i.e., measures that make it difficult to respond in the affirmative).

In Table 6, it is evident that the utilization of different operational indicators produces wide variation in the percentage of the electorate who meet evangelical criteria: only 12.5 percent of Protestants and Catholics meet evangelical criteria in the *CT* survey, while 40.6 percent do so in the Unchurched American study. Because these two studies were conducted at about the same time, it is apparent that measurement differences, not substantive differences, account for the variation between the two surveys. If low-salience respondents are dropped, the disparity between the two studies is lessened somewhat, but the differences are still great. Of particular interest are the studies where exact over-time comparisons can be made—namely, the 1964 and 1981 Anti-Semitism studies and the 1980 and 1984 voting studies from Michigan. Such comparisons over time reveal that the percentage of evangelicals declined somewhat between 1964 and 1981 (from about 22 to about 19 percent). On the other hand, the Michigan data (which used different measures) indicates an increase in the percentage of evangelicals over the past few years. Gallup, using yet another combination of measures, also shows similar increases in *Religion in America*.

It is readily apparent from Table 6 that diversity in measurement leads to differences in results. In terms of doctrinal measurement, we feel most confident in the results of the *CT* survey—in which only 12.5 percent of the total population of Protestants and Catholics fall within the evangelical category. Note, however, that this "refined" measure leans heavily toward a measurement of an "extensive" array of orthodox Christian beliefs. Obviously, measurement strategies based upon some minimal number of doctrinal beliefs might inflate the percentage. Similarly, an analysis of evangelicalism in terms of some subcultural rather than some doctrinal framework might also change the percentages significantly. However, even if evangelicals represent only 10 percent of the electorate, they nevertheless constitute, as would any large bloc of voters, a politically important segment of the electorate.

Tables 7-11 analyze the social composition of evangelicals. Table 7 compares and contrasts the composition according to different operational measures of evangelicals in which blacks are included. The distinction between conversional and confessional categories of evangelicals evident in the tables has already been discussed. The category of evangelicals labeled "parallel" evangelicals represents an attempt to create a measure of evangelicalism that best parallels the measure employed in the Michigan studies. (For a description of the operational definitions of conversional, confessional, and "parallel" evangelicals employed in the *CT* and *The Evangelical Voter* surveys, see Appendix C). Tables 8-9 present the resulting composition among whites according to the types of evangelicals and according to different surveys over time. Basically, the data reveal (1) that conversionalist (or "born again") evangelicals tend to be somewhat younger and more southern than their confessional counterparts and (2) that regardless of the measure employed, evangelicals tend to be somewhat older and less well educated than nonevangelicals, and as a group they contain a larger proportion of women and southerners (see Tables 8, 9, and 10).

The fact that conversionalist evangelicals tend to be somewhat younger than confessional evangelicals may suggest that older segments of American society may have been less susceptible to an emphasis on "born again" experiences than younger segments, which have grown up in an era in which an emphasis is placed upon experience, pleasure, and subjectivity. On the other hand, however, since conversionalist evangelicals also tend to be more southern than confessional evangelicals, it may suggest that the social meaning of the "born again" language may vary across both geographical regions and across generations. Older respondents may understand the "born again" terminology within some "instanteous conversion" framework, whereas younger and middle-aged respondents may interpret such language within some other social framework (e.g., whether one perceives oneself to be a committed Christian).

Moreover, while evangelicals do tend to be slightly older than nonevangelicals, such differences do not approach statistical significance during the 1980s. And, while it is true that a significantly low percentage of evangelicals are found among that proportion of the electorate that has had some college education, such differences are not significant within the younger (17-34) segment of the electorate (see Table 11). Consequently, the relative size of the evangelical segment of the electorate is not likely to diminish significantly in the future either by means of attrition due to natural biological processes or by increased levels of education among the younger segments of the electorate.

Religious Characteristics. Tables 12-17 analyze the religious practices of evangelicals. The data patterns evident in the tables reveal not only that evangelicals tend to be more "religious" than nonevangelicals (see Tables 12, 14, 15, and 16), but that conversionalist evangelicals tend to be more "religious" than confessional evangelicals. Conversionalist evangelicals were more likely than confessional evangelicals to report reading their Bible daily, to attend church weekly, to tithe, to classify themselves as charismatics, and to report the gift of speaking in tongues (see Table 14). On the other hand, conversionalist evangelicals were slightly less likely than confessional evangelicals to classify themselves as fundamentalist and were somewhat more likely than confessional evangelicals to watch and evaluate favorably religious television programming (see Table 13).

One further observation perhaps should be made. The data presented in Table 15 suggest that church attendance among non-evangelicals appears to have dropped precipitously from the level evident in 1964 to that found among nonevangelicals in the late 1970s and the early 1980s. The reasons for this drop are unclear, but one possibility is that many nonevangelicals have abandoned the norm of church attendance.

In Table 17, we look at differences within evangelicalism on the basis of doctrinal and experiential differences. The confessional group meets all of the evangelical criteria developed in Table 5, but the group's members are not "born again." Second, there is a "born again" group that does not meet charismatic or fundamentalistic criteria. The pure charismatic evangelical classifies oneself as a "pentecostal or charismatic," and responds to the authority of the Holy Spirit when "testing your own religious beliefs."[6] Fundamentalist evangelicals hold to a literal interpretation of the Bible, respond to the authority of Scripture when testing their religious beliefs, and believe in a personal Devil. Finally, there is a group of "born again" evangelicals who meet both charismatic and fundamentalist criteria. Data on nonevangelicals are presented to facilitate comparisons. Unfortunately, the number of respondents in many of the categories is very small; obviously, in order to investigate such differences among various evangelical groups with some precision, one needs a different sampling strategy.

Nevertheless, the data do reveal some interesting differences. Such groups do appear to be different in terms of socio-demographic characteristics (e.g., the confessional and pure charismatic groups are the oldest in age composition, while the other three groups of evangelicals tend to reflect the age characteristics of nonevangelicals). But it is particularly in terms of religious practices that interesting differences emerge. With regard to a large variety of items tapping religiosity, there is a tendency for fundamentalists to rank high and confessional Christians to rank low. It is on these measures that the differences within evangelicalism cry out for fuller examination and analysis. Unfortunately, given the already small numbers of individuals surveyed in each category, such an analysis is not presently feasible. Nevertheless, the data do suggest that both fundamentalism and "born again" experiences heighten religiosity beyond that displayed by confessional Christians. Moreover, there appear to be some

---

6. For a more detailed comparison and contrast of the political views of evangelical and charismatic Christians, see Corwin Smidt, " 'Praise the Lord' Politics: A Comparative Analysis of the Social Characteristics and Political Views of American Evangelical and Charismatic Christians," paper presented at the annual meeting of the American Political Science Association, Washington, D.C., 1984.

"additive" effects when the two are joined (i.e., those respondents who are "born again," fundamentalist evangelicals tend to be more "religious" than "pure fundamentalist" evangelicals or "born again" evangelicals; see Table 17).

Life Satisfactions. Of all the studies we have examined, only the Connecticut Mutual Life Insurance Company survey called "In Search of Values for the '80s." measures life satisfaction in any degree of depth. This survey examined various areas of life: leisure; work; relationships with friends, spouse, and family; religion; and life as a whole. In Table 18, we compare mean scores on these measures for four groups: evangelical Protestants, evangelical Catholics, nonevangelical Protestants, and nonevangelical Catholics. Although all four groups have mean scores on all the items that are in the very happy to happy range, it is the evangelical Protestant group that is the most satisfied, followed by the small group of evangelical Catholics. These findings are interesting and lead one to speculate that it might be the evangelical faith that is the cause of such satisfaction. Again, future research efforts might well pursue this possibility.

Political Attitudes and Orientations. Evangelicals not only constitute a sizable segment of the American electorate but they also tend to hold distinctive political attitudes—at least with regard to social issues and international affairs. On questions related to the role of women in society, prayer in public schools, abortion, government aid to minorities, and cooperation with the Soviet Union, evangelicals were significantly more conservative in their issue positions than were nonevangelicals in both 1980 and 1984 (see Table 19). On the question of defense spending, no significant differences existed between evangelicals and non-evangelicals in 1980, and both evangelicals and nonevangelicals adopted less conservative stands in 1984 than they had in 1980. However, the change among evangelicals was much less than that evident among nonevangelicals; by 1984 evangelicals were adopting a significantly more conservative stand on matters of defense spending than nonevangelicals.

Only on matters of economic policy do differences between evangelicals and nonevangelicals appear to be marginal in nature. On questions relating to reduction in governmental services and governmental guarantee of jobs, for example, the issue positions adopted by evangelicals did not differ from those adopted by nonevangelicals, regardless of the year analyzed. It may be that the relative support given by evangelicals for more liberal economic policies, given their lower socioeconomic position in society generally, is based upon calculations of personal self-interest. Obviously the data suggest that if economic issues were paramount in the minds of both evangelicals and nonevangelicals in terms of their voting decision, no differences in voting patterns between the two groups would be likely to emerge. However, previous research has demonstrated that evangelicals are more likely to base their vote choice on social issues than the rest of the electorate.[7] So it would not seem that this lack of differentiation between evangelicals and non-evangelicals on economic issues necessarily contributes to a lack of differentiation in voting preferences between the two groups. On the other hand, though, the data also suggest that should economic issues become highly salient for evangelicals, the voting patterns among evangelicals would likely come to reflect more closely the pattern found among nonevangelicals.

Nevertheless, the mean scores reported in Table 19 are measures of central tendency. They do not reveal the diversity evident among evangelicals. In Table 20, we analyze the policy preferences of evangelicals using data from *The Evangelical Voter* (data, you will recall, that are drawn from more highly educated, registered voters). It is evident from the table that the evangelical community, despite its conservative tendencies, is far from a monolith in its political and social attitudes. Many evangelicals hold issue positions at variance from those held by the most publicized segment of American evangelicalism, the Christian right. Given the heterogeneity apparent in the data, it would appear that doctrinal explanations of political attitudes among evangelicals are likely to be insufficient, and this opens up the question of what alternative explanations might be useful.

Tables 21-24 analyze the partisan and ideological orientations among evangelicals. Several patterns are evident in the data presented in these tables. First, given their issue positions generally, evangelicals are much more likely to classify themselves as conservatives than as liberals (see Table 22). Because different questions were used for tapping the ideological orientations of the respondents, exact comparisons across time and across studies cannot be made. Nevertheless, it is evident within each of the studies that, regardless of question format, evangelicals are much more likely to see themselves as political conservatives than as political liberals.

Second, it is evident that at least prior to 1984 evangelicals did not differ significantly from nonevangelicals in terms of their partisan self-images. Evangelicals in the Anti-Semitism study of 1964, the *CT* study of 1978-79, the Connecticut Mutual study of 1980, and the Michigan

---

7. See Jeffrey Brundy and Gary Copeland, "The Religious Vote: The Effects of Fundamentalist Attitudes on the 1980 Presidential Election," paper presented at the annual meeting of the Midwest Political Science Association, 1980; and Corwin Smidt, "Born Again Politics: The Political Behavior of Evangelical Christians in the South and Non-South," in *Religion and Politics in the South: Mass and Elite Perspectives*, ed. Tod Baker, Robert Steed, and Laurence Moreland (New York: Praeger, 1983), pp. 27-56.

study of 1980 were somewhat more partisan than nonevangelicals in that they were less likely to label themselves as Independents (see Table 22). But while evangelicals were nearly as or slightly more partisan than nonevangelicals (Tables 21 and 22), a plurality of evangelicals classified themselves as Democrats; the percentage of Democrats found among evangelicals in 1980 was nearly 10 percent greater than the percentage of Republicans (39.7 percent versus 29.9 percent respectively).

By the end of the 1984 presidential campaign, however, change had occurred in the partisan self-images of evangelicals and non-evangelicals alike. The 1981 Anti-Semitism data herald this change. Early in the Reagan administration, partisan identifications appear to shift from the 1980 levels. Shifts occurred for both nonevangelicals and evangelicals, but were greater for the latter. The 1984 data suggest that the gains noted in 1981 had been sustained within both evangelical and nonevangelical ranks. However, the pattern of the aggregate change was different for evangelicals than it was for nonevangelicals. The net Republican gain among nonevangelicals was associated with a net loss of self-classified Independents, but the net Republican gain among evangelicals was associated with a net loss of self-classified Democrats. Consequently, while a plurality of evangelicals in 1980 labeled themselves Democrats, a plurality of evangelicals in 1984 classified themselves as Republicans.

The nature of change in the partisan orientations of evangelicals is more clearly shown in the analysis of partisan affections shown in Table 23. Partisan affections are analytically and empirically distinct from partisan self-images and partisanship in voting behavior, and changes in partisan affections can be linked to subsequent changes in partisan self-images.[8] As can be seen from the table, the distribution of such affections among nonevangelicals in 1980 differed in only a few categories. First, the proportion of polarized Democrats (positive affect toward the Democratic party, negative affect toward the Republican party) among nonevangelicals (14.9 percent) was nearly double that among evangelicals (7.9 percent). Second, evangelicals were more likely than nonevangelicals to express amplified patterns of partisan affection— that is, while they ranked one party more positively than the other, they ranked the opposing party favorably as well. Slightly more than 34 percent of the evangelicals in 1980 held positive feelings toward both political parties, while 25 percent of the nonevangelicals did so. Nevertheless, overall, evangelicals in 1980 tended to divide their affects between the

8. See Corwin Smidt, "The Dynamics of Partisan Change in the United States," paper presented at the Annual Meeting of the Midwest Political Science Association, Cincinnati, 1981; and "Partisan Affections and Change in Partisan Self-Images," *American Politics Quarterly* 12 (July 1984): 261-282.

two parties: the percentage of evangelicals expressing greater affection for the Democratic than the Republican party in 1980 was nearly equivalent to the portion expressing greater affection for the Republican than the Democratic party.

However, by 1984, things appear to have changed. First, there appears to have been greater polarization within the American electorate as a whole. Among both evangelicals and nonevangelicals, there was an increase in both the percentage of polarized Democrats and the percentage of polarized Republicans, but particularly among the latter. Second, while there was a definite shift to Republican partisan affection among evangelicals and nonevangelicals alike, such a shift was more pronounced among evangelicals than nonevangelicals.

In other research not presented here,[9] it was evident that such changes in partisan affections among evangelicals were particularly pronounced among younger evangelicals. Thus, it may be that a particular generation of evangelicals, regardless of geographical region, may be undergoing a process of alignment with the Republican party—and that much of this alignment is based not only on positive feelings for the Republican party but is also associated with "hostile" feelings toward the Democratic party. Moreover, such polarized patterns of Republican partisan affection evident among young evangelicals would seem to be less susceptible to partisan change in the foreseeable future than would have been the case had their patterns of Republican affection been associated with some degree of positive affection for the Democratic party as well.

This combination of findings concerning partisan identification and affection is particularly significant. First of all, both evangelicals and nonevangelicals have moved toward the Republican party in the 1980s in terms of partisan self-image, but the greater movement has been made by evangelicals. Second, the partisan affection data suggest that both evangelicals and nonevangelicals have adopted a "polarized Republican" position—that is, they like the Republican party and dislike the Democratic party. This trend, like the trend in partisan self-image, is more pronounced among evangelicals. What is most significant, however, is that the trend is greatest among the young—and particularly among young evangelicals. Is the disaffection with the Democratic party on the part of the young simply a function of disappointment with President Carter combined with current satisfaction with the economy (as is commonly perceived), or does it relate to other issues that might attract younger evangelicals? These data do not answer the question, but they do

---

9. See Corwin Smidt, "Evangelicals and the 1984 Election: Continuity or Change?" paper presented at the annual meeting of the Society for the Scientific Study of Religion, Savannah, 1985.

make it clear that evangelical disaffection with the Democratic party is greatest among young voters, the very group Republican party leaders would most like to "capture" for purposes of winning future elections.

While evangelicals may be moving toward greater support for the Republican party, there is no clear evidence that evangelicals are moving toward increased support for the Moral Majority. When asked specifically about the Moral Majority, evangelicals tended to be divided in their position (see the bottom of Table 24). When asked about their evaluation of "evangelical groups active in politics, such as the Moral Majority," evangelicals tended to be more positive—but far from unanimous (Table 25). Similarly, evangelicals were clearly divided over which political goal they most desired; in fact, when confronted with this broad policy question, the responses given by evangelicals in 1984 closely mirrored the responses given by nonevangelicals at that time (see top portion of Table 25).

The Falwell Program. As Table 25 suggests, evangelicals were generally positive concerning "evangelical groups active in politics, such as the Moral Majority," while nonevangelicals were basically negative. But what about the policy positions advocated by Falwell and the Moral Majority? Table 19 provides some evidence to answer this question.

However, to analyze the question further, we constructed a composite measure of political positions Jerry Falwell says in his writings that he supports. This composite measure was constructed from data in *The Evangelical Voter* because its policy questions were more extensive than those in the Michigan surveys. This composite measure allows us to examine the sources of support for Falwell's policy positions among evangelicals. Table 26 presents bivariate correlations between the so-called Falwell platform and other variables. The variables in the social/demographic package behave as expected: older, less educated, low-income southerners are more likely to favor the Falwell platform than their younger, better educated, richer northern counterparts. In addition, males are more likely to support the Falwell platform than are females, particularly females who work outside the home. In terms of religious variables, there is a strong relationship between support for the Falwell platform and affiliation with fundamentalist denominations, born-again status, fundamentalist self-classification, religiosity (church attendance, etc.), and the perceived importance of religion for political choice. Moderate relationships are found with a measure of biblical literalism, while no relationship is found with an item tapping pastoral political activism. In terms of social/political attitudes, we find that the Falwell platform is strongly related to attitudes toward Jerry Falwell himself—but much less so toward the Moral Majority. Relationships are low with attitudes toward the evangelist Billy Graham and the fundamentalist publication *Sword of the Lord*. In addition, strong dislike for the Catholic Church is related to high scores on the Falwell platform. Support for the index is highest among conservatives and Republican party identifiers.

Multiple regression is a technique that examines the relationship between a number of independent variables and a dependent variable to see which of the independent variables best predict the dependent variable, while simultaneously controlling for the impact of the other independent variables. In this instance, it allows us to see which of the independent variables in Table 26 do the best job of predicting high scores on the Falwell platform and also to see which variables "wash out." We present the regression in Table 27. Only variables that reach the .05 level of statistical significance are included in the table. Among social/demographic variables, we find that old age and male status are associated with high scores on the Falwell platform, while socioeconomic status and regional variables wash out. Fundamentalist denominational ties as well as doctrinal, self-classification, and experiential measures of fundamentalism are closely linked to the Falwellian ideology, as are religiosity and the salience of religion for politics. Among social/political attitudes, identification with Falwell, dislike for the Roman Catholic Church, and a composite measure of support for conservatism and the Republican party are useful predictors as well.

Some of the implications of the findings of Table 27 are instructive. First, the Falwell platform does not attract the support of young white evangelicals, and certainly there is little evidence that the platform attracts the support of young people outside of the evangelical camp. Another growing segment of society, women employed outside the home, also tends to oppose the Falwell platform. On the other hand, there are close ties between religious fundamentalism and the Falwell ideology, and there is some evidence for the growth of fundamentalist denominations.[10] However, broadening the base beyond fundamentalism to include less fundamentalistic orthodox Christians may not be easy (although these data suggest that the avenue to accomplish this task is religiosity and its close companion, religious political salience). Moreover, the dislike of the Roman Catholic Church evident among evangelical supporters of the Falwell platform will likely be a deterrent to recruitment of Roman Catholics to the movement. And, finally, too close an identification with one of the political parties can become a liability (note the dilemma of blacks within the Democratic party).

In another analysis not presented here, attempts have been made to assess the impact of the Falwell platform on levels of political activity and

---

10. See Dean Kelly, *Why Conservative Churches Are Growing* (New York: Harper & Row, 1977).

voter preference.[11] The Falwell platform is associated with levels of political activity, but the ties are not as great as they are with variables such as ideology, partisanship, and socio-economic status. This finding is significant. Given the fact that the Falwell platform draws its greatest support from segments of the society that are traditionally low in voter turnout rates, the finding that there is a positive relationship at all between the index and rates of political activity is some indication that the efforts by Falwell and the Moral Majority to encourage participation are paying off. In terms of voter preference, it is not surprising to find that high scores on the Falwell platform are closely associated with a Reagan vote in 1980 and Reagan preference in 1984.

What are some of the implications of these findings? Among white Protestant evangelicals there is a core of support for the Falwell platform. Not surprisingly, however, that support is concentrated in the fundamentalist wing of the evangelical community. Support is much less widespread among evangelically oriented Catholics and almost absent among evangelical blacks (data not shown). The unanswerable question, of course, is whether the movement can broaden itself beyond its present base. The anti-Catholicism of the movement's core supporters presents one problem. Other problems include the old age of the core supporters, the concentration of support among fundamentalists, and the tendency of the movement to identify very closely with the Republican party, despite its southern roots.

Yet there are some hopeful signs for those who support the platform. Among those for whom religion is central in their lives, support for the movement is high. These are people who can be reached in their congregations—but only if their pastors can be activated. There is some evidence that political changes are taking place among previously apolitical Southern Baptist ministers.[12] And the future of any movement for moral reform may have some possibilities: America, it seems, is turning more and more to moral issues as many of the pressing economic problems of the past seem somewhat settled.

It is instructive to compare the findings on partisan change with those on the Falwell platform. While young evangelicals are being attracted to the Republican party, we find that these same young people are not attracted to the Falwell platform. This lends some credence to arguments that it is satisfaction with the economy and opposition to the

---

11. See Lyman Kellstedt, "The Falwell 'Platform': An Analysis of Its Causes and Consequences," paper presented at the annual meeting of the Society for the Scientific Study of Religion, Savannah, 1985.

12. See James Guth, "Political Activism among a Religious Elite: Southern Baptist Ministers in the 1984 Election," paper presented at the annual meeting of the Scientific Study of Religion, Savannah, 1985.

performance of the Democratic party under Carter that are bringing about the change. In other words, evangelical young people may be moving to the same drum beat as nonevangelicals.

Church-State Relations. Tables 28 and 29 present data concerning the position of evangelicals on questions relating to the role of religion in politics. It is evident from Table 28 that evangelicals are much more likely than nonevangelicals to feel that their leaders and organizations should make public statements on ethical/moral and political/economic matters as well as to lobby with Congress for legislations that they favor. Conversional evangelicals are more likely to hold these views than are their confessional brethren. We suspect that evangelicals would not have been so favorable to political activity two or three decades ago and that these data reflect important changes in the willingness of evangelicals to be involved in the political process. Although there is division within evangelicalism over the Falwell platform and other issues, there are subgroups of evangelicals ready to be mobilized that probably were not so inclined before. At the same time, however, it must be recognized that religious considerations may represent just one factor among many that influence the political decision making of evangelicals. While evangelicals take this religious factor seriously, it does not necessarily represent an overriding factor in the formulation of their voting choice. Rather, it may well represent just one factor that is given equal consideration with various other factors in such decision making (see Table 29).

Social Justice. Table 30 presents data concerning the position of evangelicals and nonevangelicals on questions relating to matters of social justice. Obviously, some of the questions presented in the table tap more directly than others the issue of social justice. Nevertheless, each of the questions involves some relationship to different aspects of social justice, and taken together they provide a broader portrait of the perspective of evangelicals and nonevangelicals on such matters.

Do evangelicals lack a social conscience? Not necessarily. When asked "Do you think that society as a whole has an obligation to see that children, the handicapped, and the elderly have their basic needs met?" evangelicals were just as likely as nonevangelicals to respond that society does have such a moral obligation. Given the manner in which the question was posed, it is perhaps not too surprising that nearly everyone, evangelicals and nonevangelicals alike, agreed that society has such an obligation. However, there is also some indirect evidence in Table 30 suggesting that the social conscience of evangelicals is as strong as if not stronger than the social conscience of nonevangelicals. When asked what they as individuals should do about poverty in their community, evangelicals were less likely than nonevangelicals to respond that they had no obligation to do anything beyond paying taxes.

Rather, it would appear (although the pattern is not totally clear) that evangelicals tend to be more attuned to the individualistic ethic than nonevangelicals. For example, evangelicals were more likely than nonevangelicals to state that they would respond to poverty in their community through personal and direct help or through religious and community organizations. Nevertheless, when asked what source should provide for societal needs, evangelicals mirrored non-evangelicals in stating overwhelmingly that it should reflect some combination of governmental and voluntary efforts (though the exact mix of the two may be different in the minds of evangelicals and nonevangelicals).

Political Participation. Evangelicals constitute a relatively large segment of the American electorate and hold distinctive political views. Yet on the basis of these characteristics, evangelicals as a social group have only potential importance politically. Two other factors affect the relative importance of evangelicals politically: their level of political activism and their cohesion in voting behavior. Given the social/demographic characteristics of evangelicals (low status, female, southerners), we would expect lower turnout rates over time for evangelicals than nonevangelicals. In Table 31 we compare turnout rates over time for evangelicals and nonevangelicals. Note the expected lower turnout rates for evangelicals are evident in the 1960s; however, by 1980 evangelicals were voting at rates as high or higher than nonevangelicals. It should be remembered that, given their socio-demographic characteristics, evangelicals should not be participating at rates as high as nonevangelicals. Moreover, many evangelicals have been part of a cultural tradition that has eschewed political participation. Obviously, something has brought about a change. Among the possibilities are the Carter candidacy, a widespread perception that traditional values are collapsing and immorality is increasing, the emergence of a conservative political movement, the candidacy of Ronald Reagan, and the development of the Christian right. Whatever the explanation, these data on turnout rates for evangelicals need further exploration.[13]

Also included in Table 31 are rates for other forms of participation. It is apparent that evangelicals continue to trail nonevangelicals in all nonvoting forms of political participation. This particular pattern, how-

---

13. For a beginning of such an exploration, see Corwin Smidt, "Evangelicals versus Fundamentalists: An Analysis of the Political Characteristics and Importance of Two Major Religious Movements within American Politics," paper presented at the annual meeting of the Midwest Political Science Association, Chicago, 1983; and "The Mobilization of Evangelical Voters in 1980: An Initial Test of Several Hypotheses," paper presented at the annual meeting of the American Political Science Association, Chicago, 1983.

ever, appears to reflect a stage that tends to be common among emergent political groups. First, emergent groups tend to trail dominant groups in all forms of participation. During the second stage, emergent groups begin to depart from their nonpolitical ghetto. During the third stage, they begin to reflect the dominant groups in their levels of voter turnout but continue to lag behind in their level of other forms of political participation. At the final stage, they participate at rates equal to the dominant groups in society. Evangelicals do not appear to have reached this final stage, but they may have arrived at the third stage. Regardless of the particular stage, evangelicals appear to have come a long way politically since the early 1960s.

In Table 32, we find data similar to that examined in Table 31 except that all whites are examined rather than white Protestants and Catholics only. More importantly, however, in Table 31 only those respondents who said that their religion provides "quite a bit" or "a great deal" of guidance in their everyday life were included as evangelicals, while in Table 32 such a requirement was dropped. Note that voting turnout for evangelicals in 1984 is 70.1 percent in Table 32, but is 75.4 percent in Table 31. Moreover, Table 32 suggests that the turnout rate among evangelicals in 1984 fell below that found among non-evangelicals, while Table 31 suggests that it remained the same. Clearly, it is the high-salience evangelicals that made turnout rates so high in Table 31. Which table has the most appropriate conceptualization of who should be classified as an evangelical? We leave it to the reader to judge. The point is this: how one conceptualizes and then measures evangelicalism makes a big difference in one's substantive findings.

Voting Behavior. Tables 33 and 34 analyze the voting patterns of evangelicals and nonevangelicals with regard to elections for national political offices. Table 33 analyzes changes in such voting patterns between 1980 and 1984, while Table 34 analyzes changes in presidential voting only across a variety of different studies. It would appear from Table 33 that while white evangelicals seem to have voted more Democratic than white nonevangelicals in 1976, they have subsequently voted more Republican than nonevangelicals. Such Republicanism in voting among evangelicals is evident not only in presidential elections but also in congressional and senatorial elections (despite the fact that a large proportion of evangelicals reside in the South).

Because Table 34 includes data from the Anti-Semitism study of 1981, it restricts analysis to white Protestants and Catholics. The same general patterns noted in Table 33 are also evident in Table 34. But the data presented in Table 34 further suggest that evangelicals may always have been more Republican in their presidential voting than non-evangelicals: the data from the 1964 Anti-Semitism study reveal both higher Republican voting among evangelicals than nonevangelicals in

1960 and higher projected Republican voting among evangelicals than nonevangelicals in 1964. However, several points caution against reaching such a conclusion too quickly. First, the anti-Catholicism evident in the 1960 Kennedy-Nixon campaign would have been much more significant among evangelicals than nonevangelicals, and so the level of support for the Republican candidate among evangelicals that year was likely unrepresentative. The projected presidential vote for 1964 would seem to support this conclusion. Second, the operational measures employed in the 1964 study tend to reflect the criteria of "confessional" rather than "conversional" evangelicals—and since conversional evangelicals are more likely than confessional evangelicals to reside in the South (see Table 8), the 1964 Anti-Semitism study may not adequately reflect the greater Democratic voting likely to be evident among such southern evangelicals.

In the end, then, we cannot speculate with any certainty about the voting patterns evident among evangelicals prior to the mid-1970s. But we tend to believe (1) that there likely were important regional differences in the voting patterns evident among southern and nonsouthern evangelicals and (2) that, while regional differences still persist, they have diminished over the past several decades. If such is the case, then there is greater cohesion in the voting behavior of evangelicals today than in the past. And, at least in the short run, such increased cohesion enhances the political clout of evangelicals as a voting bloc.

Yet, in the long run, there may be some distinct disadvantages in aligning too closely with a particular political party. If, as James A. Reichley suggests, "the most important service churches can offer to secular life in a free society is to nurture moral values that help humanize capitalism and give direction to democracy,"[14] then churches that align themselves too closely with a particular political party may eventually come to be perceived by the general public as mere appendages to transitory political factions and hence as less morally credible.

CONCLUSION

Several major conclusions can be drawn from this general survey. First, it is evident that evangelicals constitute an important bloc of voters, a bloc that holds distinctive views politically and that over the past decade has displayed increased politicization and cohesion in its voting behavior. While this increased politicization and cohesion may have been associated with movement toward increased Republicanism, evan-

---

14. Reichley, *Religion in American Public Life* (Washington, D.C.: Brookings Institution, 1985), p. 359.

gelicals continue to remain a somewhat heterogeneous group in terms of their political views, partisan orientations, and voting behavior.

Second, it is evident that this analysis tends to concentrate on doctrinal measures of evangelicalism because of the nature of the data available. Such concentration on our part does not imply a commitment to this approach as the best method of examining the evangelical phenomenon. After all, doctrinal criteria do not lead to homogeneity on the part of evangelicals in terms of their social and political attitudes, partisanship, levels of political activity, and voting preferences. On the other hand, this is not to say that religious variables have no impact on these attitudes and behaviors. It simply means that we have not clearly identified whether or in what manner religious variables do play a role. It is here that understanding how historical and subcultural factors interact with doctrinal essentials is so important. And, it is also at this point that religious worldviews and self-identification with the evangelical movement may lead to an explanation of differences in the political attitudes, orientations, and behaviors evident among evangelicals.[15]

Third, it is evident that evangelical scholars need to develop better measurement strategies in identifying evangelical respondents through survey research. Evangelical scholars have at times tended to dismiss survey research, leaving the development of questions, the analysis of data, and the distribution of findings to nonevangelical scholars. Such scholars frequently lack even a basic sensitivity to fundamental analytical distinctions in the development of such questions and the analysis of subsequent data. By leaving the task to nonevangelicals, evangelical scholars foster both the formulation and perpetuation of gross misunderstandings concerning the role of evangelicals in contemporary politics.

Finally, it is evident that there is a need for periodic and continuing national and local surveys on evangelicals. Such surveys will likely have to be funded by evangelical bodies and be devised and analyzed by a community of evangelical scholars. Present research is totally dependent upon the few questions available through the various surveys reviewed here. As a result, our understanding of the nature of those who fall within the contemporary evangelical movement and how they react to the world about them continues to remain somewhat unclear.

---

15. On religious worldviews, see Peter Benson and Dorothy Williams, *Religion on Capital Hill* (New York: Harper & Row, 1982); on self-identification with the evangelical movement, see Marsden, *Evangelicalism and Modern America*; and Lyman Kellstedt and Corwin Smidt, "Defining and Measuring Fundamentalism: An Analysis of Different Conceptual and Operational Strategies," paper presented at the annual meeting of the American Political Science Association, New Orleans, 1985.

ent the Canisius College Financial
Directions on how to apply and
e included with the application
o the gold pages of the Viewbook
ous financial aid programs.

ur college search. We encourage you
f our campus. To arrance an appoint-
0, ext. 204 or 205, or outside the
dents may dial toll-free 1-800-435-
Monday through Friday.

you soon!

The Story of an Encounter

Michael Cromartie

What does biblical obedience require of political thought, especially in the context of the American democratic experience? If evangelicals and fundamentalists could have more power in the political arena, what would they do? And would it be good for American democracy? These questions were discussed by twenty-two evangelical historians, philosophers, political scientists, and activists gathered for a two-day invitational conference at the Billy Graham Center on the campus of Wheaton College in Illinois. The moderator and convenor of this important discussion was Richard John Neuhaus, the director of the Center on Religion and Society in New York City.

In his introductory comments, Neuhaus outlined the purpose of the conference: to assist the reconstruction of a religiously based public philosophy. "Evangelicals and fundamentalists in America, together with others of course, are going to contribute to this reconstruction," he said, "or it is not going to get done." Noting that there has been much reflection by evangelicals and fundamentalists on the necessity of political involvement, Neuhaus observed that the more urgent question remains: How does biblically empowered political engagement strengthen or challenge democratic principles?

Neuhaus stressed the importance of the conference by reminding the group that there are many in the political, cultural, and religious leadership elite of American society who are "scared to death" by the conservative religious insurgency in the political arena. "They are not at all convinced that this is not bad news for the liberal democratic experiment" and therefore "many of these people feel forced to side with the

Norman Lears and the ACLU factions in our society out of a felt terror at the prospect of an antidemocratic or potentially oppressive authoritarian insurgency in the public arena."

While the participants agreed on viewing the Bible as the final authority for all matters both public and private, it was anticipated that there would be a diversity of opinions on how theological principles should be applied in our present social and historical context. Expecting such, Neuhaus urged the group to make special efforts to "really hear one another" and to listen responsively. Moreover, he shared his hope that we would "achieve some good disagreement." He reminded us that the great Jesuit scholar John Courtney Murray was fond of saying that "disagreement is a rare achievement, and most of what is called disagreement is simply confusion." As can be seen from the discussion that follows, some good disagreement was achieved and, accordingly, some confusions were clarified.

I. EDWARD DOBSON SESSION

Neuhaus introduced Dr. Ed Dobson, an active leader of the Moral Majority (now the Liberty Federation) and a teacher at Liberty University in Lynchburg, Virginia. Dobson, who has been teaching at Liberty for fourteen years, described himself as an "unbiased fundamentalist" and an active participant in what he calls "politicized fundamentalism." He described politicized fundamentalism as a loose-knit coalition aiming to combat the increasing secularization of society. The movement was stimulated by the *Roe v. Wade* Supreme Court decision, the gay rights movement, and the removal of prayer from the public schools. Dobson sees a parallel between the fundamentalists of the turn of the century who banded together to fight theological liberalism and the politicized fundamentalism that began to emerge in the late 1970s. The one principal difference between the earlier fundamentalism and today's is that contemporary fundamentalists are willing to form coalitions—not only with other conservative Christians but with Jews, Mormons, Catholics, and anyone who shares their common moral concerns and social agenda. Dobson noted that it was in 1976 that Jerry Falwell realized how much potential there was to influence the political process. After Jimmy Carter's *Playboy* interview, Falwell publicly disagreed with President Carter on his TV program. Falwell, much to his surprise, received a call from Hamilton Jordan on behalf of Carter requesting him to refrain from such comments and to please "back off." Falwell was startled that his comments would cause such concern and came to perceive the incident as his "initial baptism" into the world of politics, the incident that led to the founding of the Moral Majority in 1979.

Dobson highlighted two points from his paper (all of the papers appearing in this volume were sent to participants in advance of the conference to facilitate the discussions) that are of primary concern to fundamentalists regarding social and political involvement. First, a commitment to evangelism and the Great Commission. Dobson explained that this is their overarching concern: "Political and social involvement is secondary to our compelling and consuming desire to get people saved. We want to bring all of the nations under the discipleship and authority of Christ." Second, the command of Christ to be "light and salt" in the world should inexorably lead Christians to exhibit their concerns for their neighbor in every level of society.

Dobson concluded his introductory comments by reminding us that we live in a fallen world and, given the various political options we have, "democracy seems to be the best option."

THE DISCUSSION

Moderator Neuhaus initiated the discussion by posing this question: Does God require democracy? Is democratic governance theologically mandated? Before discussing the question, Neuhaus explained his reason for asking it. When we say that there are certain theological principles that are very important concerning how a society ought to be governed and also realize that democratic societies are the most respectful of those theologically mandated principles, what does this say about democracy?

Dobson confessed that he was hesitant in responding to these questions but agreed that theological principles and historical evidence seem to indicate that "democracy is the best direction." His chief concern was to be sure that the church and state were seen as separate entities. Ronald Nash of Western Kentucky University interjected that, as an amillennialist, he is struck by the correlation between the presbyterian form of government in the early church and a representative form of government. Ronald Sider of Eastern Baptist Theological Seminary argued that it is a combination of biblical principles and analysis of history that lead him to conclude that "democracy is perhaps the best way to go now in this fallen world."

Mark Noll of Wheaton College joined the discussion, questioning whether "fundamentalism in principle can present an answer to the sort of question that has been raised." Referring to the "ready-fire-aim" metaphor used in Dobson's paper to describe fundamentalism in general, Noll noted that if fundamentalists are in principle people of action first, then they simply cannot answer the question of whether the system they are in is theologically more appropriate or not. He went on to say, "If the process is always to act and then justify action, then the kinds of questions we are asking about the theoretical, theological justification for democracy simply cannot appear; there needs to be a whole other area of inquiry on work, labor, etc. to develop a kind of theological perspective on activity in the public sphere." If fundamentalist political activity is based on certain principles, he added, they must not be "unexamined principles."

British author and theologian Os Guinness picked up on Noll's point. When non-Christian observers look at the evangelical movement, he noted, one of their most important observations is the "lack of a Christian mind." "We have seen fundamentalism move from an uncritical pietism," said Guinness, "to an uncritical activism in politics." Dobson admitted that fundamentalists constitute "a movement of paradoxes," but he said that he used the "ready-fire-aim" metaphor to emphasize a different point: the urgency to get involved. "We just didn't call together a hundred fundamentalist leaders and educators, and say 'Now let's look at the Bible and see how what we believe about the Bible should govern what we are now going to do in the political process.' We just simply got involved in the process."

At this point Richard Mouw of Fuller Theological Seminary raised some objections to the course of the discussion, arguing that for forty years in this century dispensationalism provided the fundamentalist movement with a framework and a relatively coherent social vision. Change began to occur in 1947 when Carl Henry wrote *The Uneasy Conscience of Modern Fundamentalism*, in which he rejected the dispensational framework for social action. But, despite the book's importance, Mouw suggested that Henry put forth his argument in "rather vague terms" and that it really amounts to a plea for more social involvement on the part of the neo-evangelicals than the fundamentalists had previously exhibited. Mouw argued that in terms of having a social ethic, the neo-evangelical movement floundered until the 1973 "Chicago Declaration of Social Concern," which "set off a lively exploration of different traditions." This included the beginning of *Sojourners* magazine, a search for an Anabaptist social ethics, a combination of "Thomas Merton and Dorothy Day social worker type" Catholicism influencing evangelical social thought, and different varieties of Reformed political philosophy. There has been "in the last fifteen years," Mouw said, "this intensive dialogue and exploration for a coherent perspective that can provide an alternative to dispensationalism." Now, he maintained, Jerry Falwell has come along with his "politicized fundamentalism" and basically rejected the original dispensational perspective, a lot like Carl Henry did in 1947, but he has done so in such an ambivalent way that his program, too, lacks any coherent vision. He sees the fundamentalist movement as being where the neo-evangelical movement was at the end of the 1940s, "lacking a tradition." His larger concern is that fundamentalists develop a clear political philosophy rather than "making continual appeals to the Great Commission." He wondered if there might be a "kind of neo-Thomist-Puritan synthesis" that will emerge in the development of fundamentalist political theory.

CONCERN FOR THE POOR

At this point Ron Sider asked why concern for "justice for the poor" was not a part of the original vision of Moral Majority. Tim LaHaye of the American Coalition for Traditional Values and a member of the "inner circle" that helped found the Moral Majority, agreed to speak to the issue. "A partial answer," said LaHaye, "is that we felt welfare was so out of control and harmful to the poor and that it is individuals who should help the poor." He went on to say, "We are not really convinced that it is a responsibility of government" to help the poor. "If it is, [the system] sure needs to be overhauled and made more efficient." Sider agreed that the welfare system is in need of extensive reform but stressed that it is a matter for important debate, given biblical principles, as to the amount of concern the government should have regarding assistance to the poor.

LaHaye responded by arguing that he is concerned about the "deserving poor, but assistance should be tied in with self-respect and self-training with the hope of getting people onto a self-sufficient basis." He adds, "I am not sure that government should be in the business of taxing, and if the government cannot tax there will not be enough money to help the poor. Government should provide a haven and a protection so that individuals can help the poor, along with churches."

This comment met with strong disagreement from Nicholas Wolterstorff of Calvin College. There is an important distinction between charity and justice, he insisted. "As I read the long history of Christian tradition, it says that the poor have a claim on us, that they have rights, that a society is obligated to set up institutional arrangements which will ensure not only that people are not clubbed over the head but that they are not ground into poverty." Wolterstorff added that it is not just a question of "well-intentioned people running soup kitchens" but an obligation of the state to see that justice is done to the poor.

AMERICA: A CHOSEN NATION?

Turning to a different issue, Neuhaus asked if there were any significant actors in the evangelical/fundamentalist political initiative in American life who believe that "America is in some theologically serious way a chosen nation or that America participates in a covenantal relationship with God and his purposes in history unlike other nations." Ed Dobson immediately responded that Jerry Falwell is often accused of holding this position, but in fact this is not the case. Falwell understands the phrase "the Christianizing of America" to mean the "reemphasizing of those values that are represented by the Judeo-Christian moral system," said Dobson. "I know that he is not claiming it to be the chosen nation above all other nations." Tim LaHaye agreed, noting that the only person he knows who holds such a position is Dr. Rousas Rushdoony.

Richard Mouw pointed out that the reference to "my people" in 2 Chronicles 7:14 ("if my people who are called by my name humble themselves, and pray and seek my face, and turn from their wicked ways, then I will hear from heaven, and will forgive their sin and heal their land," RSV) is often assumed by certain fundamentalists to apply automatically to the United States. Such proof-texting, Mouw suggested, is an implicit endorsement of the "chosen nation" theme. Dobson disagreed, arguing that "the underlying presupposition is that if we honor God's standards, then God will bless us. It is an individual promise, a family promise, and applies to any nation equally."

George Marsden, now at Duke Divinity School, noted that President Reagan in his speech to the National Association of Evangelicals convention said that America is good and prosperous and a very special place. Marsden said he finds this a very pervasive and popular opinion in America. James Skillen of the Association for Public Justice added that he is concerned about the attempt to identify nations as somehow equivalent to a people of God. He said that he cannot find any biblical basis for such a view, and he urged that "we should not talk of the nation here as a potential people of God, because the only people of God that the New Testament allows is the worldwide church of God in Christ."

This met with strong agreement from Richard Mouw. This, he said, is an important issue for those from the Reformed community who take 1 Peter 2 seriously: the church is a "holy nation" and the "new Israel." "Through the blood of Christ there is a new kind of nationhood being created that at best 'relativizes' all other national identities," said Mouw. "The Christian has two kinds of nationalism: one is the nation of blood-washed sinners drawn from every tribe, tongue, people, and nation of the earth. That is our primary identity. Then out of that we decide how we are going to handle our life among the Gentiles and the Gentile nations in the sense of the present geopolitical entities; but this is so overridden by that sense of being a blood-washed citizen of the kingdom of Jesus that it creates a tension."

Dean Curry of Messiah College did not disagree with this, but he urged that we avoid two extremes. One extreme, he suggested, is to say that "the United States government is ordained of God and therefore ipso facto every foreign policy of the United States is also ordained of God." On the other hand, we should avoid the extreme which says "I am a citizen of the kingdom of God and therefore the United States and every policy it pursues is seeking to achieve goals and objections that run contrary to the kingdom of God." Curry concluded by reminding us that being a member of the "transnational body of Christ" does not mean that we do not have "earthly" loyalties to those in our own nation and to those around the world.

I momentarily abandoned my role as *rapporteur* to suggest that underlying this discussion is the problem of "moral equivalency," the view that as superpowers the United States and the Soviet Union are moral equals. One does not have to be a blind "God and Country" patriot to be concerned about the failure on the part of the "evangelical left" to make clear distinctions between democratic governments and the practices and intentions of totalitarian regimes. The continual practice of standing "over against" one's own democratic government—however flawed—because of a commitment to being a citizen of "another kingdom" can lead to politically irresponsible judgments in the geopolitical world.

George Marsden wondered at this point whether there are any evangelicals who are inclined toward the "blame America first" syndrome. There might be some, he said, who, because they are Americans, feel "a special responsibility to point out American mistakes that they would not have of some other nation," but he doubted that there are any in the evangelical community who say that "America is the primary source of evil in the world." Ron Sider agreed, adding that he doesn't believe the "radical evangelicals" are guilty of this, although they are often accused of being anti-American. "I think," said Sider, "we need to be very careful when we suggest that there are some folks around in the evangelical community who want to see the United States as somehow worse than other nations."

At this point Neuhaus confessed his doubts about this line of argument. Abandoning his role as moderator, he joined the discussion.

> It seems to me that clearly there are evangelicals, *Sojourners* for example, who will explain that the Sandinista's clampdown on civil rights and on all political rights now in Nicaragua has essentially the United States to blame. They will say that the Soviet Union has put in such and such missiles in reaction to aggressive policies here or there, that the Ethiopian government was not helpful with regard to relief because of legitimate fears of United States designs, etc. Now this is what I take is meant when people talk about the "blame America first" syndrome—that is, one explains injustices in the world by references *first* to America.

Sider conceded that there has not been a "full balance, and I wish there had been." However, he did not feel the description of *Sojourners* given by Neuhaus is accurate. Said Sider, "the intent has been to say we must criticize what we are a part of first, because this is where we have a democratic responsibility." Neuhaus noted that this brought us back to our earlier discussion of how Christians should "order their loyalties" with respect to their life in this community called America. "I just find it interesting," Neuhaus remarked, "that some people have ordered their loyalties in ways I do not fully understand and they clearly intend to be very strongly Christianly motivated in that ordering."

Reentering the discussion, Richard Mouw reminded us that the late William Stringfellow, in his book *An Ethic for Christians and Other Aliens in a Strange Land*, had a "blame America first" tendency. He said "America is Babylon" and frequently referred to the "American Way of Death." Mouw argued that the "young evangelicals" appropriated the theology of "principalities and powers" with a new understanding of "demonology." The "major demons identified were so often ones that they saw as most at home in North America, such as militarism, consumerism, and all the rest. So there was this mentality that tended to see the worst principalities and powers as having the United States especially in its grip."

FIDELITY AND BLESSING

At this point Nicholas Wolterstorff wanted to reintroduce a subject that was mentioned earlier. He was curious about the connection that Dobson and LaHaye have made concerning "fidelity and blessings," saying that he finds the implied connection very dangerous. "It sounds as if we can assume that God is going to bless those nations and individuals who are faithful. The flip side of that is the nation or individual which finds itself in suffering—that is a clue to infidelity." He strongly disapproved of such reasoning. "I don't think the Bible allows us to say that. Those who suffer are not necessarily disobedient. There are perhaps tiny little nations in the world who are relatively impoverished who are living more faithfully than the wealthy ones."

Tim LaHaye was clearly puzzled by Wolterstorff's comments and argued that "the promises of God in Proverbs and Psalms are promises even of long life to those who observe his principles." Wolterstorff challenged this: "But there are also the psalms of lament and they bear roughly equal weight with the psalms of praises. And the lament is this cry out to God, 'Why do the wicked prosper?' And characteristically, the psalms of lament do not say that the root of the deliverance for which the person is crying out is wickedness on the part of the person. I think we have to hold out the possibility that down throughout the ages there have been faithful individuals and nations that have been relatively faithful that did not enjoy prosperity. It just seems unbiblical to make that quick equation."

Os Guinness then reminded us of the early Puritans, in whose era some of these issues have their origin. The English Puritan William Perkins clearly said that there was not always a direct link between "prosperity and blessings." He made it very clear that it is a much more complex issue. Guinness pointed out that Perkins often cautioned that prosperity could be the result of "God's blessing, God's testing, God's judgment, or the devil's temptation." Ron Sider agreed, noting that there are "a host of biblical texts which say that the rich often get rich by oppression. There are more texts of that sort than there are texts which say the rich are rich because they are obedient." He contended that both assertions are valid, and he wanted to affirm them both, but he was concerned that the "folks who talk about the fact that 'we are rich because we have been obedient' tend not to talk about the other." Neuhaus was sympathetic with Sider's view on this point, but he also suggested that those who talk much about the acquisition of "unjust riches" very seldom talk about "riches as a just recompense for righteousness."

James Hunter, a sociologist from the University of Virginia, wanted to take a closer look at the whole issue of the "selective reading of Scripture" and its implications for the discussion. "My observation as a social scientist," he said, "is that what we have in terms of method is both the extreme right and the extreme left doing exactly this: they provide ex post facto legitimation for a political agenda that has already been set and derived from other sources. This ex post facto legitimation is looking through Scripture to find biblical justification for a different agenda."

WHAT THE FUNDAMENTALISTS WANT AND THE PROBLEM OF RHETORIC

George Marsden mentioned that he often receives questions from journalists who want to know "What do the fundamentalists really want? What would the nation look like if they had their way?" He reported that he tells them there are two strands of thought in the history of fundamentalism. There is a strong tradition for the separation of church and state, and there is another tradition that would like to see an official establishment of religion. He asked participants for their observations.

Responding to Marsden, Tim LaHaye confessed that some of "our own people don't really know what we want, but generally, we want what most Americans want, which is moral sanity." He went on to say, "We do not want coercively to force people to believe, . . . but we do not think that in the area of public education the American people should be indoctrinated with the religion of secularism, which is a minority viewpoint anyway."

Ed Dobson suggested that Marsden's questions are difficult to answer because of their hypothetical nature. "Our first allegience," he maintained, "is to the church and not to the state, and consequently I don't think we have a desire to control the state, the government, the school, or any other social structure in our society." He admitted that fundamentalists do have a desire to "influence" society and to make sure "our view is represented." One of the motivating factors for the founding of the Moral Majority was to create a "vehicle through which our views could be represented in the broad rainbow of pluralism in our country."

But Marsden pressed further. "Suppose you could really have control and power, would it really be pluralistic?" Dobson replied, "I would hope that it would be. It seems to me you lose the whole essence of Christianity when you try to impose it on people." And to this Tim LaHaye added, "This fear of fundamentalist control is a fear of the imagination."

Os Guinness pointed out that the more the fundamentalists' positions are clarified, the less threatening these positions are to people. He cited Rabbi Haberman of Washington, D.C., as an example. The Rabbi has said that he found in conversations with Jerry Falwell that almost all of his fears were a matter of the "carelessness of rhetoric" on the part of the fundamentalists and that virtually all of his fears have been removed. According to Guinness, the disagreements over policies underlying many moral-political issues in America are not substantive but rather "procedural, as to how faith and public policy should relate in the first place." It is here that much of the careless rhetoric causes confusion, he said. Guinness granted that the problem is not simply rhetoric—there are very important issues in the background—but when the carelessness of rhetoric is removed, we find that "the procedures are not that far apart, and while you will have terrific differences in the substance, the procedures will be brought closer."

In closing this lively session, Neuhaus wondered aloud if it were not apparent to each participant that most of the anxieties that have been expressed in the larger culture could be eliminated in large part by simply "clearing up our language and becoming more lucid about what precisely it is that people are saying they want."

II. JAMES SKILLEN SESSION

In his introductory remarks, James Skillen of the Association for Public Justice in Washington, D.C., made it clear that he believes the fundamental starting point for Christian political philosophy is biblical revelation. Says Skillen, "We are required to ask what God has intended his creation to be, and we must make a continuing systematic effort to see what the Bible demands."

Skillen reminded us that all governing of society through political institutions implies an imposition: all political authorities impose something. Our concern should be to see that justice is done in our kind of complex society. This means devising answers to important questions. What is a just state in the modern world? Which issues are appropriate to the political community, and which are not? To come up with the answers, he said, we need a public philosophy that precisely defines what a government ought to do and that bases our notions on biblically normative grounds. Skillen contended, for instance, that in the Moral Majority there is no public philosophy that clearly spells out what the role of government should be. Getting a majority of votes for a given policy change does not make it right, nor does it provide an argument as to why such a policy is just.

THE DISCUSSION

James Hunter began the discussion by saying he wanted to test the limits of the "confessional and structural pluralism" that Skillen refers to in his paper. "It seems to me that the problem of the religious right is a reaction not to confessional pluralism but to moral pluralism. How much pluralism are you willing to tolerate in your model here? For instance, how would you handle abortion pluralistically?"

Skillen replied that there are certain life-and-death matters that cannot be handled pluralistically. Abortion ought not to be subject to a pluralistic argument, for example. The same is true of traffic laws: you have to agree to drive on the right side or the left side of the street, and everyone must drive at certain agreed-upon speeds. You cannot have pluralism there. In the case of such life-and-death matters, Skillen said, the very nature of the identity and life and existence of a citizenry demands "public judgment" and government responsibility. However, he also argued that in responding to a diverse community with its plurality of religious faiths and diversity of educational options, "it is incumbent upon the public authorities to see that the public law does justice to everybody that is going to be involved. If you have a community that is highly diversified through all kinds of forms of life coming in, I don't think it is the job of the government to try to eliminate it or make it homogeneous."

Richard Neuhaus suggested that a point of critical clarification was needed concerning how the term *pluralism* was being used here. When most people speak of pluralism, they are referring to a "kind of monism of indifference and a libertarian 'do your own thing' idea which, I would say, is the opposite of pluralism." Skillen's type of pluralism, Neuhaus suggested, is "a structural pluralism where God's governance is in fact pluralistically exercised with the state being one of the agencies of governance. So it is not a libertarian proposition but rather a proposition about the pluralistic distribution of governmental authority in societal life."

Tim LaHaye found this discussion unsettling. He wondered if pluralism is not actually a "secular humanist concept" that was brought in historically as a secularist ethic to help accommodate the Judeo-Christian ethic "so both can live here happily." He argued that the Bible has distinct guidelines for the purpose of government, which according to 1 Timothy 2 is to conduct a society in such ways as to have peace, quiet, godliness, and reverence. "It seems clear to me," LaHaye said, "that that is the New Testament purpose of government, and when it doesn't function that way it produces civil confusion that leads to anarchy." He explained that this is what he means when he says he would like to see people in office with a commitment to "moral sanity." Such people would ensure that we would have peace and quiet in our community and reverence for God.

Skillen saw in LaHaye's perspective a misunderstanding of pluralism. He argued that pluralism, as a matter of principle, is precisely an effort to find a biblically obedient means of doing what God calls people to do. Skillen granted that very much of early America can be accounted for only against the backdrop of the Western Judeo-Christian tradition, but he pointed out that the separation of church and state was developed historically out of the conviction that the very attempt to gain control by force in order to impose one faith in a diverse and pluralistic society is what perpetuated the religious wars and crusades. That, Skillen added, "wasn't peace and quiet." Having an established church, he argued, "is a confusion, because the state does not exist to reinforce a particular church."

It is not the responsibility of the government, for instance, to tell people how to raise their families. "Some parents must be allowed to let their children study what they want for their children. The moral conscience I want the legislator to have is an ability to say 'It is right that parents should be respected in the raising of their children; schools ought to be respected in their independence; and the churches ought to be respected.'" A well-ordered, just society allows people "freedom of conscience" to raise their children according to their traditions and customs. Allowing such freedom does not make one a moral relativist, Skillen asserted. "I want to have the kind of schools that I can send my children to that will not be neutral and that will teach them the way I want them to learn. But if I want that, then I need to have from the government's point of view the same right for every other parent."

Richard Mouw responded that such an outlook looks good on paper, but he is uneasy about the "growing plurality about which we are trying to be pluralistic." Mouw finds it ironic that right around the time evangelicals and especially Calvinists begin talking about pluralism and toleration in healthy terms, "it almost seems like the wrong time to be doing so." He expressed a concern that the "fact of plurality itself seems to contribute to an atmosphere of relativism." He noted, for example, how the fostering of an atmosphere of plurality and respect for different viewpoints has caused young people who have grown up in a strong Dutch Calvinist school system to be suspicious that their own viewpoints might not be true because "there are so many other viewpoints around." This makes childrearing, for instance, more difficult in the area of doctrinal and theological education. But more specifically, Mouw wondered if we have gotten to the place where the specific viewpoints about which we are called to be pluralistic are so bad that "it is hard to sort them out in terms of a norm of justice." He referred to the growth of dangerous cults, Satanic worship communities, and new religions with other horrible practices. He passionately argued that such communities should not be allowed to exist. It is not clear how to apply a norm of justice to these new movements, he admitted; nonetheless he is concerned that "Satanic cults and incest-practicing communities do not become things that we ought to be widening the pluralistic net for."

"I don't think those kinds of communities ought to exist either," Skillen said, "but I don't want to ask the government to simply disallow certain communities that I don't like because I know there are people in this society who think certain charismatic groups should not exist either." The larger question comes back to what constitutes the appropriate use of authority and the need to discern when this authority does too little and when it does too much. Moreover, Skillen voiced his concern about what the consequences would be if the government tried to keep certain kinds of communities from existing. His guess is that they would find a way to live underground. But more importantly, there would be an even greater skepticism about the government's ability to perform its legitimate and limited role.

James Jordan of Geneva Ministries in Texas remarked that "we are giving an uncertain sound in the marketplace when the late Francis Schaeffer writes in a book that he wants a Christian Republic on one page and wants pluralism on the next." Jordan asked Skillen to expand on how broad a definition of pluralism he had in mind.

Skillen replied, "The pluralism for which I am arguing is what I think is a Christian view of society"—that is, the separation of church and state is an example of the kind of imposition that does justice to our plurality of faiths this side of the kingdom of God. He explained that he takes this imposition to be a Christian view of political order. If there is a dangerous religious cult that promotes child sacrifice, say, as a part of its rituals, the government should prohibit it from actually engaging in such sacrifices, provided it does so on the grounds that it has the responsibility to protect life and not simply because it doesn't happen to like that peculiar religious faith. It is the duty of the government, said Skillen, "to exclude certain kinds of practices" in order to protect life and recognize the rights of all citizens, including the unborn.

At this point I again entered the discussion to observe that it is often fundamentalists who are accused of not understanding pluralism. But is this really the case? It seems those most confused about the true meaning of pluralism are the members of the American Civil Liberties Union and the editors of the *New York Times*, who excoriated Archbishop O'Connor for speaking out against Geraldine Ferraro's position on abortion.

Neuhaus concurred, suggesting that even the language of pluralism and compassion has been monopolized by one sector of American society. Their opponents have played into their hands, however, letting them use these words in a way that totally distorts the reality. The language is inescapable in that there is no way in which any movement that isn't democratic, pluralistic, and tolerant is going to go anyplace in America. But the words are going to have to be redefined, especially with regard to the media. If we look at three movements that have had an enormous impact in the last twenty or thirty years, said Neuhaus—the civil rights movement, the feminist movement, and the evangelical resurgence—almost no one denies that the last is as significant in its impact on American life as the others. Yet the media elite has felt an obligation to understand and sympathetically interpret the first two—the civil rights and feminist movements—while "there wasn't even a suggestion at the *New York Times* editorial board that this should be the response to the fundamentalist movement and its insurgency in the public square," said Neuhaus. "It is truly dramatic, and it was instinctual that this movement was seen as the enemy."

This line of argument proved a little puzzling to Richard Mouw. "I seldom watch television," he confessed, "but when I do I see evangelicals and fundamentalists explaining their views quite often." And the same is true concerning the print media, he said: "I see an amazing influx of evangelicals giving religious commentary in the secular media and there are more and more evangelicals being asked to comment on issues. I see a concerted effort to broaden the scope, so where am I missing your point?"

Neuhaus contended that with the civil rights movement and the feminist movement there was a deliberate effort on the part of the media sympathetically to explain these movements to the American people. These movements were seen as an expansion of democratic pluralism, whereas the fundamentalists and evangelicals have been treated as a threat to the media's vision of how America ought to be. Neuhaus granted that fundamentalism and evangelicalism are getting a lot of attention, but largely through their own fault they are getting attention for seeming to be antidemocratic and antipluralistic. "Until we can turn that around," he warned, "I think we are going to see increasingly this polarized and sterile opposition in our culture and in our religion."

Nicholas Wolterstorff agreed with Neuhaus on this point but suggested that there is more to it than an unfairness on the part of the media. He thinks Tim LaHaye is right when he says the intelligentsia in this country are profoundly antireligious. To understand American society, we need to take account of the division between the roughly ten percent of the American people who constitute the intelligentsia and the remaining ninety percent who on the whole are not antireligious. The ten percent by and large run the media and write the textbooks. Their inability to understand and explain evangelicalism is rooted in "the story that these Western intelligentsia have told themselves about humanity's odyssey for two centuries now," said Wolterstorff.

> They have said to themselves that it is the destiny of humanity to shuck itself of religion, and when humanity becomes mature, then it will become irreligious. And so there is the tale that secularization is an almost inevitable process, and what goes with that is the notion that religion is an epiphenomenon that doesn't explain anything. You explain it, but you don't use it to explain anything. So the civil rights movement may explain something and feminism may explain something, but evangelicalism doesn't explain anything; it needs explaining. Furthermore, it is a throwback to the childhood of the human race, and so forth.

As long as the Western intelligentsia "tells itself that tale," Wolterstorff argued, it will not only misunderstand what goes on in American religion but will also misunderstand what goes on in the rest of the world.

Corwin Smidt of Calvin College wanted further clarification from Skillen on his view of how a "Christian state" would be ordered: "The way I understand it, you could talk about this Christian state without there being any Christians living in it. Isn't it true that your discussion focuses primarily on procedural matters?" Before Skillen replied, James Hunter offered a similar observation: "It seems to me you are defining justice procedurally and not substantively. You are defining justice as a technique, as a methodology for dealing with conflict."

Skillen countered that "there are important procedural characteristics of a just state in terms of due process, electoral procedures, structural diversity of protection for education, etc., and to me those are very substantive and not just procedural. The government must structurally do justice to what is not a part of itself. It does not create churches, it doesn't create families, and that is a very substantive statement about what the government ought to be doing."

At the end of this session, Neuhaus asked Skillen for summary comments. Skillen responded that he is concerned that Christians not become just another interest group in Washington but instead get a clear understanding of what the task of the government should be and how that is grounded in a deep conviction about the meaning of life in this world. His purpose in his paper was to argue for a just state and to show how the government can do justice by correctly addressing the plural structure of our society. We need clear convictions about what precisely the public order ought to be, he said, and we should enter political life with our "full confessional identity intact." If Christians do not get these fundamental principles clear, he concluded passionately, "I think it is all up for grabs, it is hopeless, and I think the political process is at its end."

Neuhaus noted that Skillen's concern summarized the reason for our meeting: "What a tragedy it would be, of the proportions of a last chance lost, if thirty years from now people looked back at that time in which 'politicized evangelicals and fundamentalists' were no more than momentarily one more powerful interest group that the brokers of power had to take into account for a while until they split apart again and went back to the wilderness. Unless we help change the meaning of politics, we have not made the contribution we have been called to make." On this point there was no disagreement.

III. RONALD SIDER SESSION

Before elaborating on his paper, Mennonite theologian Ronald Sider commented that the overall slogan for the position he represents is what he calls a "consistent pro-life stance." He does not think we should get our ethics for public life from some general version of natural law but instead from biblical revelation. Christians need a new vision, a "redemption ethic" that starts, epistemologically, with "what God's revelation says is good." We cannot have a satisfactory social ethics unless we "listen to every part of biblical revelation and develop a normative paradigm that reflects the full flow of the biblical disclosure."

Sider reminded us that while God has called us to be coworkers in the process of shaping history, we should have "modest expectations about bringing in the kingdom." It is our task to "create modest improvements or avoid worse things." We need to have a "biblically balanced agenda," and this includes making economic justice for the poor a part of the political agenda of Christians. Sider wanted to emphasize that, rumors to the contrary notwithstanding, he is not a socialist and does not believe the state should own the means of production in society. "But it does seem that the Scriptures say that economic justice in the social order is one of God's very important concerns, and we must be as concerned about this as the Bible is."

One of the characteristics that will issue from a biblically balanced lifestyle will be our nonconformity to the surrounding culture, Sider contended; conformity has been "one of our greatest temptations through the centuries." As Scripture so often emphasizes, we must be challenging the way things are rather than "cheering on the culture." If our public policy proposals simply reflect the culture rather than Jesus and the Scriptures, then no matter how much influence we have, we will not be fulfilling the role God has for us. Today, said Sider, evangelicals are "so deeply conformed to the culture in conscious and unconscious ways that the impact is going to be largely insignificant."

Concluding his introductory remarks, Sider expressed a deep concern about the "tone and character" of the internal debate among evangelicals and fundamentalists on matters of public policy. He cited several recent books that have created a "vicious debate that could tear us apart and cause us to self-destruct." Vigorous debate is needed, he said, but it is absolutely crucial that disagreements be articulated correctly and honestly. "We need to be careful, in a new way, to state each other's positions in a way that the other person says 'Yes, that is really what I mean—when you attack that position, you are critiquing the substance of what I'm wanting to say.'" Continual misrepresentation and distortion of each other's views will cause us to miss important opportunities.

THE DISCUSSION

Our moderator expressed his gratitude to Sider for the reminder that we need to learn more and more the "obedience of responsive hearing of one another, making sure we are not bearing false witness." However, Neuhaus added, "we should not fudge the fact that it is a hard thing to understand civility as a religious virtue and at the same time say there is a war going on and you have to take sides on some very basic issues." The struggle comes in discerning how to take sides and prosecute one's case as effectively as possible while remaining in the bonds of civility and, more importantly, in the bond of Christian community.

EVANGELICALS AND INERRANCY

Ed Dobson began the discussion with a comment about the inerrancy of Scripture. As a fundamentalist, his concern is that before he has a working relationship with evangelicals he will need some assurances that they have the same belief about the Bible that he does. He feels it important that we start with the same presuppositions about the Bible, and so he wanted to know Sider's view on inerrancy. Sider responded that he is a member of the Evangelical Theological Society and regularly signs in good conscience their statement affirming that Scripture is inerrant. He added that "the Scriptures themselves are the Word of God written, and they are my norm; everything that they intend to teach I believe and want both to affirm and to live." Dobson pressed further: "Is the Bible without error not only in matters of religion but in science, history, and the cosmos?" Sider replied that the inerrancy statement of the Evangelical Theological Society is intended to leave room for those who say that it may be that the Scriptures are not intending to teach this or that specific point about a geological statement, for instance.

Richard Mouw wanted to know why Dobson raised the question. "We can talk about flood geology," said Mouw, "but that is an entirely different conference."

> I have never sensed in any place in our discussions on social, political, and economic matters that any of us has ever been in-clined to say that "this verse that deals with the state, or our obliga-tions to the poor, is in error." I have not sensed that there are those of us whose disagreements are based on somebody else taking a part of the Bible as true where we want to say it is in error. The question of inerrancy does not arise in our discussions on these issues. For instance, I was once at a meeting at the National Council of Churches and we were discussing the issue of homosexuality and I said "What do you do with Romans 1?" and the guy said "I don't read it—I don't like Paul." Now that is a confrontation over whether God's Word is true. But I have never sensed at an evan-gelical/fundamentalist discussion that that was the kind of issue, where someone would say "I don't like Amos." So I wonder why that should be an important item of discussion here. Is it because Ron raised some issues and you would prefer to stop the discussion at this point rather than deal with the issues?

No, that was not the case, said Dobson. On the left wing of evan-gelicalism he sees a "dangerous tendency for people to take on the word *evangelical* and have it mean more than historically and theologically it ought to mean. I am glad to hear what Ron has said on this issue."

THE TONE OF THE DEBATE

Ronald Nash was interested in Sider's concern about the "tone of the debate" and wanted to offer his perspective on why this debate has be-come so shrill. The shrillness started, he argued, with "a spate of left-wing evangelical books in the early seventies." Speaking personally, Nash explained that one of the reasons he got involved in the political process was his own growing anger at what he saw as the unfairness of the "evangelical left's" attacks on conservatism.

We were heartless, cruel, materialistic, and all that crap that came out of those books. So forgive me, but the guys on the left started it. Then *Sojourners* started out as the *Post-American* and that influential cover of the *Post-American* that I will never forget with Jesus in Pilate's judgment hall draped in an American flag with an essay inside on the "bitch goddess of capitalism." If you want to know why I'm involved in political and economic matters, you can trace it back to that particular issue of the *Post-American*.

Historian Mark Noll called for a "point of order" at this point. "You have to read the *Christianity Today* editorials of the 1950s and 1960s to understand why that language was the way it was. I defend neither, but we've got to set the historical record straight."

Nash went on to contend that "those of us on the right are looking for some signals of openness and fairness toward conservatives." But in his ongoing review of *Sojourners*, he said, he has "found everything but that." He concluded by urging Sider to write an essay for *Sojourners* that "opens a door" and "holds out a palm" to show that there are some fundamental and important values on which we agree. "Let's start sending signals to each other," he said.

Ken Myers, formerly of *Eternity* magazine and now editor of *This World*, also expressed some concern about the character and tone of our internal debates. It is important that we be "honest with each other as we try to be civil but not conceal what are very serious disagreements in the interest of civility," he said. In the interest of politeness, Myers asserted, "evangelical elites are guilty of a kind of tokenism. There are times when we may have to say clearly that this position is fundamentally wrong and problematic and dangerous. Within the bounds of civility we must remember that in Scripture error is condemned seriously." Myers added that there are some ideas that are "just plain ridiculous, and I am not sure that ridicule per se is un-Christian behavior." Sider replied that his norm is not civility but truthfulness: "People's positions should be presented fairly and in a way that the other person says 'Yes, that is what I believe.'"

Neuhaus added that we should all "agree that we ought not bear false witness—that is absolute. We should not be mean-spirited, and we should not impugn motives." He also expressed a wish that people "would not use *civility* as if it were a wimp word, because it is a vibrant, vital word."

Mark Amstutz suggested that it is extremely important that we "depersonalize the debate, because we are debating policies and not personalities. It is immaterial *who* says something; the issue is the moral legitimacy of the policy being proposed." Our arguments, he said, are about policies, not people. George Marsden concurred, commenting wryly that "We have a special gift of incivility in our communities in the way we treat each other, and we therefore should not try to cultivate incivility."

Richard Mouw noted that evangelicals and fundamentalists have a special problem with rhetoric because "it is a very real part of our history." We have been nurtured on a "strong spiritual-warfare kind of thinking." We enlist people to gain popular support for our cause, and consequently rhetoric takes on a special role in our appeals. But he said that he has seen some encouraging signs recently:

> There is a new emphasis on shared goals. It is very important, and I don't think it is just rhetoric. I am deeply grateful to the Lord for the neoconservatives because for the first time in a long time, a lot of us are saying we are concerned about the poor. Michael Novak says "We are concerned about the poor." Ronald Nash says "We are concerned about the poor." Never again can it be said that Ron Sider is on the side of the poor and these other people are pushing something else. There is a common goal. How are we going to do it? What best delivers? A lot of that is empirical stuff that we have to look at. We have to become very critical of our own economic assumptions. And those of us who have been using leftist rhetoric have to be very honest about the fact that we are very aware of the horrors of socialist societies and the evils that have been brought about there.

IS NEO-CONSERVATISM A TREND?

It had been suggested both in Sider's paper and in our subsequent discussion that perhaps the new conservatism in the country is the dominant cultural consensus in America today. It had also been suggested that if this is the case, then evangelicals must be careful lest they be "conformed to the surrounding culture" by following the policies that are currently fashionable. Dean Curry of Messiah College had some objections to this line of thinking and argued that it stretches the imagination to believe that neo-conservatism is fashionable among America's elite.

> Where is it fashionable to be a neo-conservative? Among college and university faculties? Among actors, artists, and writers? Among the media and journalists who write and report the news? I am afraid not. If we are talking either numbers or influence, the fact is that those with left-leaning sympathies still dominate the media, the academy, and the arts in this country. Now my point

here is first of all that it is incorrect to make this dominant cultural argument, because the dominant culture is not neo-conservative. Second, it avoids the central and crucial issue of the substantive arguments made by the neo-conservatives themselves. I am asking that we closely examine the reasons and the substance of the arguments that these people are making. It is just not good enough to dismiss their arguments as a reflection of the dominant culture and hence fashionable. Most of these people have broken ranks at great expense.

Sider responded that he "only means to be saying that we must be careful, if we are swinging with different changes in the culture, to ask ourselves who is setting the agenda." Os Guinness asserted that a much deeper issue is involved here. We must ask ourselves, said Guinness, whether we are "really consciously and self-critically distant at any moment from whatever is the dominant culture. In biblical language, we are all more worldly than we realize. Or to put it in Peter Berger's language, we can never escape the social context of our coming to know things. Always and inevitably we are more bound by social context than we are aware of." Guinness granted that we are all working and living in different places, but he said he is concerned that we ask ourselves where we are in relation to the dominant movement of the day and then be sure we keep a self-critical distance in our own thinking. "I have to say in all honesty that I don't see among my Christian neo-conservative friends the willingness to distance themselves in their thought. How do we know that neo-conservatism has taken a wrong turn today? Because nothing is more certain than that in twenty years' time neo-conservativism will be as washed out as sixties liberalism is now."

Dean Curry responded that he only wishes that Jim Wallis or perhaps even Ron Sider would see that many of the assumptions that they begin with also reflect what in reality is the dominant cultural opinions of the leadership elite of America. At this point I again took the liberty of entering into the discussion to comment on Guinness's observation that neo-conservatism is but a passing trend similar to the liberalism of the sixties:

There is no doubt in my mind that in the next ten or twenty years neo-conservatives may disagree on domestic issues—about how best to help the poor through a limited welfare system or what the immediate structure should be. But what I do not think will change in the next twenty or forty years is the fact that sixty million people have died in Soviet Gulags, a million people are dying in Afghanistan, people have been slaughtered in Cambodia, there is political oppression in Cuba, Bulgaria, Eastern Europe, North Korea, and around the globe. All of these things are intractable historical facts that will not go away. When the former editors of *Ramparts* magazine say they have become neo-conservatives, they are doing this not on the basis of domestic issues or cultural trends but on the basis of geopolitical realities that have caused them to say "We are tired of the brutality and the genocide."

Neuhaus reminded us that part of our biblical obedience requires a careful reading of history and sharing with one another our readings of history. Neuhaus then suggested that perhaps we could agree that the comments Curry and I had made were aimed at suggesting that part of being in favor of democracy entails being unapologetically and intelligently anticommunist. On this we all agreed.

CONCERN FOR A CHRISTIAN PUBLIC PHILOSOPHY

Our moderator pointed out that we had not yet dealt with a question that deserved a lot of attention:

> How do we move as evangelical Christians from a Bible-based Christianly empowered political concern to language and argument in the public arena that is genuinely public in character and that can engage people who don't care about the Bible and who are not Christians? They must be able to understand that what we are talking about is justice, which we say is mandated by God but which is not limited to those who care about whether or not it is mandated by God. You need not go as far as blessed Martin Luther, who said he would rather be ruled by a wise Turk than a stupid Christian—although I am prepared to go that far, because there is profound wisdom in that observation. We want to take biblical positions, but we must ask how to take biblical positions that are genuinely public in character and not limited to those who acknowledge the lordship of Christ.

George Marsden picked up on this point and put a similar question to Ron Sider: "When you go to the public arena and say 'Here is a biblical principle that the government should follow,' why should you expect a domain that has very little to do with the kingdom of God to be impressed with that appeal?"

Sider replied that while he would appeal to norms that the other person has, he would take care to guard against "setting my agenda and the Christian community's agenda by norms that are from somewhere else. That is what I am very concerned to protect." Marsden wondered if Sider doesn't really aspire to take over the state, because of his Anabaptist views, in order to implement biblical principles. "Is it an outsider's agenda that one ought to have, or would there be a possibility of getting power in order to disarm yourself?"

Sider did not presume to know the answer. "Only God knows the answer to that. What I am called to do is to keep presenting the norms of the kingdom, live them out within the church, and say to the larger society, 'Jesus Christ is Lord, and here is the way we ought to go.'"

James Jordan brought up a different issue, calling attention to a point in Sider's paper at which he says that "the state should not legislate criminal penalties for breaking biblical-ethical norms, except for those which violate the rights of others." Jordan confessed that he has "terrible reservations about human-rights rhetoric." He said he does not think our social-ethical theory "can be grounded in any doctrine of 'rights.'" He argued that we should care for the poor not because they have certain "rights" but because the "law of God commands us, and we will be judged if we don't." He finds that our concerns in law and revelation provide a surer foundation for social ethics.

Mark Noll expressed his discouragement about any possibility of evangelical consensus on the matters we had been discussing. He said he is encouraged by "advances in good will and honest discussion," but his discouragement hinges on the very "nature of American evangelicalism and the nature of how we move from belief in the authority of the Bible to positions on specific issues." He outlined at least four stages we must go through before we even get to the particular issues. First, we have a belief in the authority of the Bible but we have disagreements among ourselves about the meaning of inerrancy. Second, we have different views on how we interpret the Bible, despite all of us agreeing on its full authority as God's Word. Third, we then have the process of coming up with a theological understanding of how to put the Bible to use politically, but even in the Reformed community we have different emphases. And finally, we read social and political history differently among ourselves. And we have to go through all these stages before we get to the fifth stage of taking a position on particular public policy issues. "It is overwhelming," Noll concluded. "How can we develop even a loose coalition on public issues?"

Mark Amstutz concurred and suggested that there has been an underlying assumption on the part of evangelicals that if we have a uniform view of the Scriptures we will somehow agree on different public policy issues. Amstutz said he fundamentally disagrees with this and feels "it is very possible to agree on biblical principles and disagree on the means to achieve them. What we need is a toleration of one another on our understandings of history, and the application of social science theory to the particular public policy actions."

As this very lively session came to a close it became increasingly clear that agreements on the major premises of biblical authority obviously do not lead to agreements on the minor premises of specific public policy proposals. But there was an informal covenant about the need for a more civil rhetorical style in the vigorous advancing of our arguments.

IV. KEN MYERS SESSION

In his introductory comments Ken Myers mentioned several ideas that undergirded his paper but were not included because of space restrictions. He said he feels that evangelicals must refrain from continuing to address those "apathetic folk who are behind us" instead of engaging the "cultural elite and merchants of our culture" who influence so much of American thought.

As evangelicals develop a growing interest in public policy, Myers insisted, we need to focus more attention on the "different capabilities of the regenerate and the unregenerate" in formulating a proper political order that will accommodate them both. Myers warned that some policies put forth by those on the left and the right tend to be too optimistic about the capabilities of unbelievers to have similar concerns.

Jim Skillen acknowledged the fact of sin in our political life but said he fears that this emphasis on sin may end up turning sin into a norm. It becomes too low a standard from which to judge what public justice should be and thus runs the risk of turning selfishness into a norm. "I don't know of Marxists," Skillen argued, "who come along being convinced of what they think a proper public order is and who then say 'Well, most people don't agree with our convictions, so we will find some lower common denominator that we will operate with.' No, they come in contending for their position. It all relates to where you start with this distinction between the regenerate and the unregenerate."

Richard Mouw added that while we need to be aware of the fact of sin, "we need to promote, for instance, an economic system that allows for the possibility of the love for the poor, allows for the possibilities of self-sacrifice, and so on. We acknowledge the fact of sin but we also must acknowledge the possibility of righteousness and call for an economic system that allows righteousness to be done."

Myers agreed that we should not "determine a norm and then cut our losses." But when we do ask the question of what justice does, we need to "keep the realities of sin in that definition." We should not settle for second best when defining our norms. Myers contended that we should have no illusions about what to expect from sinful humanity, including ourselves.

Aware that Myers once worked at National Public Radio and witnessed the inner workings of this "adversarial culture," Os Guinness asked him how civil this part of our culture really is. How much of the coverage by secular reporters is unwitting in its bias and how much is genuinely malicious? Myers replied that for the most part there was a lack of knowledge rather than an outright hostility toward the faith. Guinness suggested that the "genius of the First Amendment is that it defused the need for the language of theological warfare," and he wondered aloud what would happen if we cleaned up our "language and careless rhetoric" and articulated the real meaning of principled pluralism. "Would we find the unwitting people won over because they understood us, or would there be a hard core that would not accept whatever we said?"

Ed Dobson said he was sure that there would always be a hard core of people who would "never be won over no matter what you did, short of getting out of the political process altogether and keeping your mouth shut." Guinness then asked for Neuhaus's opinion in light of his being situated in New York and having followed the *New York Times* for so many years. Neuhaus replied,

> I believe in the demonic and I believe there are people who are possessed by a hatred over which they have little control and a hatred of all that is good and true and beautiful and godly. I believe there are other people who are not in any way possessed in any supernatural manner, who have come to a conclusion, not unlike the progenitors of the secular Enlightenment of the eighteenth century, that religion is an absolutely lethal force in the public realm. It is their considered opinion that to unleash this piety in public would destroy the fabric of our civil society. They would therefore go to the death to resist what most of the people in this room think ought to happen. And that is hard-core opposition.

Before taking a break from the discussion, Neuhaus asked us to reflect on the following question: "If the evangelical and fundamentalist insurgence were ten times more effective than it is now and were to become a culturally and politically formative force in American life, would this be good or bad for the liberal democratic experiment?"

Upon our return, Os Guinness expressed concern about Christians "who are thinking only in terms of the nation-state and national interests" when they "should actually be thinking nationally as to what America's role in the world should be, and that goes beyond national interests and ideals." He further suggested that whereas Christians should be transforming this debate, by and large they are not doing so.

Dean Curry said he is not optimistic about a greater evangelical influence in political formation and in the way we govern ourselves. He cited as evidence the impact of certain politicians who are Christians in the present political order. "I am not sure that justification by faith guarantees good government and good politicians." He went on to say that

Biblical obedience and liberal democracy require more than evangelism and more than agreement on principles. What it does require more of is a more sophisticated, extrabiblical kind of reflection. It involves reflection on history and philosophy. We do not have this tradition in the Protestant church; Catholics are very fortunate in this regard. We need to spend more time examining those extrabiblical considerations and what they might demand of us.

Tim LaHaye had difficulty pondering what evangelicals/fundamentalists might do if they got in power because, as he said, "I am afraid we are not going to get in power." Neuhaus took this occasion to interrupt and underscore a point: "This is the crunch point and exactly what these two days have been about. You say you are afraid that you will not get in power, but the trouble is that there are millions of Americans out there who are afraid that you will get in power. And one of the reasons they are afraid that you will get into power is that they don't know what you would do when you are in power. One of the reasons they don't know what you would do in power is that you and all of us have not thought through precisely what it would mean for this insurgency to succeed."

"We would be delighted," LaHaye responds, "to activate the platform that Ronald Reagan went in on."

But speaking as an Englishman, Os Guinness had a larger concern.

I am deeply moved to think that one hundred and fifty years ago Britain was the leading society in the world. Evangelicals had a door of opportunity, which some of them like Wilberforce and Shaftesbury seized with great effect, but most missed, and within a generation evangelicalism went from being the most decisive influence in Victorian England to being a subculture, and it has remained that ever since. Now in an extraordinary way, America is at a turning point, and there is a cultural opening for evangelicals, among other traditions. And to me the central question is: does evangelicalism, including fundamentalism, have the integrity and the effectiveness required either by discipleship or the national or international opportunity to do what is required? That to me is the crucial question. Before the Lord at this moment we must be asking what needs to be done.

Mark Noll laid out some points in response to Guinness's concerns and Neuhaus's original question.

What is required is a combination of a defense of the American tradition, defined as the democratic experiment, and devout prayer and encouragement of the Christian virtues. Specifically, we must strengthen constitutional balances and encourage the practice of politics as public service. Second, we must strengthen economic freedoms and lay increased emphasis on the practice of Christian sacrificial charity. Third, we must emphasize American forcefulness in the world while encouraging Christian humility about our motives and increasing efforts to understand the nature and cultures of other peoples in the world. To do one without the other in any of these instances will leave us worse off than we are now.

The cultivation of "civic virtue" is lacking in the evangelical tradition, Ken Myers added, and should be taught in all of our evangelical colleges. We have a new interest in changing social structures and have always been concerned for evangelism, but there is a large area in the middle that needs more attention: the encouragement of civic virtue among all citizens.

Nicholas Wolterstorff suggested several items we need to reflect on in counseling new politically conscious evangelicals.

First, we need to reflect and act out of an understanding of the demands and promises of the gospel, not out of some natural law, not out of consensus, but out of obedience to the gospel. We need an understanding of Christian political servanthood and informed Christian minds. Second, I think we've got to hear the voices of suffering, of unfairness, and of injustice. We have got to learn to listen and become in Jesus' sense a community of mourners. Third, we have got to understand the dynamics of the modern world—and there are other dynamics besides secular humanism. Fourth, we need to continue to develop a Christian philosophy of politics. And last, we must do our best to speak civilly, and with love, and to never bear false witness.

As our discussion drew to a close, perhaps one of the most telling points came during this final discussion, when no unified agreement could be reached on exactly what we would do if we were given full power in the policy arena. Some challenging recommendations were made, but these came only after our moderator kept bringing us back to the question. As if to avoid the hard issues, we tended to keep changing the subject.

Many differences surfaced during these two days, and more questions remain. It is clear, for instance, that only occasionally have the subjects of natural law, common grace, and the place of general revelation as it applies to the democratic political process come into focus. This was cause for some conern on the part of our moderator:

One problem we have not resolved is this question of natural law and the gospel—whether or not there is a normative, morally compelling way of ordering society with a philosophy that is genuinely public, that does not assume obedience to the gospel, and does not assume Christian particularity. This, I suspect, is going to be the real crunch point in the future of this movement. Unless that is settled, I think that the people who fear that the people in this room are going to gain power are going to be, with considerable justice, motivated to fight to the death the insurgency we have been discussing, because they will not be part of it, because they don't qualify in terms of obedience to the gospel or in terms of being Christian. Unless that nut is cracked in some way, I think we are headed for religious warfare in America. I think it is not alarmist to say that this society could unravel and we would have our own version of the wars of religion of the seventeenth century.

This was a sobering note to end on, but not an altogether depressing one. A discussion of political philosophy among such diverse evangelical thinkers has rarely occurred before, and it may be that this important in-house dialogue could prompt a reconstruction, or a construction for the first time, of an evangelical public philosophy.

Tables

Table 1
VARIATION IN "BORN AGAIN" QUESTION

Study	Exact Question Posed	Percent Born Again
Unchurched American 1978	"Would you say that you have been born again, or have had a born again experience—that is, an identifiable turning point in your life?"	34.3%
Christianity Today 1979	"Have you ever had a religious experience—that is, a particularly powerful insight or awakening—that changed the direction of your life, or not?"	32.9%
	In addition: "Is this experience still important to you in your everyday life, or not?" "Was this a conversion experience—an identifiable turning point that included asking Jesus Christ to be your personal savior, or not?"	21.2%
Connecticut Mutual 1980	"Was there ever a specific time in your adult life when you made a personal commitment to Christ that changed your life?"	48.7%
Michigan 1980	"Some people have had deep religious experiences that have transformed their lives. I'm thinking of experiences sometimes described as 'being born again in one's life.' There are deeply religious people who have not had an experience of this sort. How about you; have you had such an experience?"	24.4%
Anti-Semitism 1981	"We've heard a lot in the last few years about individuals who have been 'born again'—have you personally had such an experience?"	22.4%
Michigan 1984	"Some people have had deep religious experiences which have transformed their lives. I'm thinking of experiences sometimes described as 'being born again in one's faith' or 'discovering Jesus Christ in one's life.' There are deeply religious people who have not had an experience of this sort. How about you; have you had such an experience?"	28.0%

131

Table 2
"BORN AGAIN" RESPONDENTS AND OTHER MEASURES

Item	Number	Percent of Born Again
Have not made a commitment to Christ	92	13.4%
Consider Bible a "book of legends"	38	5.7
Never pray to God	18	2.7
Not "certain" Jesus rose from the dead	118	17.4
Do not believe in the resurrection	55	8.0
Believe Jesus neither God nor Son of God	64	9.6

Table 3
COMPARISON OF "SUSPECT" AND "NON-SUSPECT" BORN AGAIN RESPONDENTS

Item	N=1256 Not Born Again	N=254 Suspect Born Again	N=452 Non-Suspect Born Again
Attended church in last 6 months	44.0%	51.5%	75.6%
Attended church at least once a week	42.7%	44.5%	65.3%
Ever not attended church for 2 years or more	44.2%	47.9%	31.7%
All/most of friends attend church	28.9%	27.4%	53.1%
Prayed twice a day or more in past week	16.9%	29.8%	46.5%
Pray at meals	22.4%	24.8%	47.1%
Pray constantly	5.5%	7.7%	27.9%
Watch religious TV or listen to religious radio	27.4%	38.3%	59.6%
Church member	49.6%	52.6%	81.2%
Active church member	49.2%	54.4%	73.9%

Table 4
COMPARISON OF SAMPLE DISTRIBUTIONS OF SURVEYS UTILIZED

	Anti-Sem. 1964	Unch. Amer. 1978	Anti-Sem. 1981	CT 1978-79	Conn. Mut. 1980	Ev. Voter 1983	Mich. 1980	Mich. 1984
Age								
18-25	29.2%	41.7%	42.3%	37.6%	41.2%	34.1%	38.1%	37.8%
35-55	39.7	30.4	29.4	32.9	*	34.4	32.0	33.7
56 +	31.1	27.9	28.2	29.5	*	31.4	29.9	28.5
Education								
Less than high school degree	47.4	29.8	19.4	27.2	31.3	16.1	25.6	21.4
High school degree	30.6	34.6	31.9	39.7	37.0	33.0	35.4	36.1
Some college	21.9	35.6	48.6	33.0	31.7	50.9	38.8	42.5
Region								
South	27.2	26.1	**	25.1	**	44.4	27.0	28.8
Non-South	72.8	73.9	**	74.9	**	55.6	73.0	71.2
Race								
White	87.0	90.7	86.1	91.0	87.6	87.1	86.8	86.4
Non-White	13.0	9.3	13.9	9.0	12.4	12.9	13.2	13.6
Sex								
Male	48.1	50.8	49.8	48.2	47.1	39.9	43.7	43.9
Female	51.9	49.2	50.2	51.8	52.9	60.1	56.3	56.1
	N=1975	N=2103	N=1215	N=1552	N=1295	N=1000	N=1408	N=1989

*Data unavailable in terms of the exact categories utilized
**No data available at all

Table 5
HOW "EVANGELICAL" IS MEASURED IN VARIOUS SURVEYS

1964 and 1981 Anti-Semitism Studies — Respondent believes that acceptance of Christ as Savior is necessary for salvation, believes without doubt the existence of God, in the actual existence of the Devil, and in life beyond death. Salience is measured by saying that religion is either "extremely" or "quite important."

1980 and 1984 University of Michigan Election Studies — Respondent has had a born again experience and believes that "The Bible is God's word and all it says is true." Salience is measured by saying that religion is "an important part of your life," *and* that it provides "quite a bit" or "a great deal" of "guidance in your day-to-day living."

1978 Unchurched American Study — Respondent believes that Jesus Christ was God or the Son of God, believes with certainty in the resurrection of Jesus, has made a "commitment" to Christ, accepts the Bible as God's literal or inspired word, and believes in life after death. In terms of salience, religion is regarded as "very important" "in your own life."

1979 *Christianity Today* Study — The respondent believes in Christ as God or the Son of God, that "the only hope for Heaven is through personal faith in Jesus Christ," that the Bible is God's word and without mistakes "in its statements and teachings," in God, in life after death, in the Devil, that God played a role in creation, that salvation is an important "personal need," and that helping "to win the world for Jesus Christ" is an important priority for Christians. Salience is measured by responding that "your beliefs about God" provide "a lot" or a "fair amount" of "consolation and help."

1980 Connecticut Mutual Life Insurance Study — Respondents must have made "a personal commitment to Christ that changed your life," rank salvation as a very important aspect of their lives, and have had a religious experience at least "occasionally." In terms of salience, respondents had to answer yes to the question, "Do you consider yourself a religious person?"

1983 Evangelical Voter Study — Respondent had to believe "that Jesus Christ was a real person who lived on this earth and who was also the unique Son of God," "to personally accept Jesus Christ as his or her savior in order to have eternal salvation and to be saved from eternal hell," or to answer positively to the question "Would you call yourself a born-again Christian — that is, have you personally had a conversion experience related to Jesus Christ?"

Table 6
PERCENTAGE OF EVANGELICALS IN VARIOUS SURVEYS*
(PROTESTANT AND CATHOLIC RESPONDENTS ONLY)

Percent of evangelicals among:	1964 Anti-Sem.	1978 Unch. Amer.	1978-79 CT	1980 Conn. Mut.	1980 Mich.	1981 Anti-Sem.	1984 Mich.
Total population of Protestants and Catholics	22.0% (1852)+	40.6% (1739)	12.5% (1360)	32.5% (1151)	18.8% (1384)	19.3% (942)	25.0% (1967)
Protestants who are evangelicals	26.4% (1341)	43.5% (1198)	17.7% (887)	40.0% (788)	24.1% (1014)	26.8% (609)	31.8% (1385)
Catholics who are evangelicals	10.6% (511)	34.5% (541)	2.7% (473)	16.1% (363)	4.3% (370)	5.7% (333)	8.8% (582)
Whites who are evangelicals	21.4% (1606)	41.6% (1582)	12.9% (1232)	31.4% (999)	19.1% (1051)	17.8% (779)	23.3% (1690)
Blacks who are evangelicals	26.3% (236)	31.3% (150)	8.3% (121)	42.6% (91)	39.5% (147)	34.5% (119)	35.5% (228)
Protestants and Catholics when low salience removed	21.5% (1851)	30.8% (1739)	12.5% (1360)	29.9% (1151)	17.5% (1384)	18.6% (942)	21.8% (1967)

*Evangelical Voter Survey of 1983 is excluded because it is intended as a sample of evangelicals only

+N's or totals in parentheses are the number upon which the percentages above are calculated

Table 7: COMPARISON OF SOCIAL COMPOSITION OF EVANGELICALS ACCORDING TO DIFFERENT OPERATIONAL DEFINITIONS OF EVANGELICALS (*Christianity Today* Survey)

	Conversionalist (Prot. only)	Confessional (Prot. only)	Combined (Prot. only)	Combined (with Cath.)	Parallel (Prot. only)	Non-Evangelical
Percentage of evangelicals	12.5%	21.0%	22.4%	29.4%	15.5%	84.5%
Age						
18-34	24.5%	24.5%	24.8%	26.0%	25.6%	39.8%
35-55	41.7	35.1	35.3	37.6	37.8	32.0
56+	33.9	40.4	39.9	36.4	36.6	28.3
Total	100.1%	100.0%	100.0%	100.0%	100.0%	100.1%
(N)	(192)	(322)	(343)	(450)	(238)	(1295)
Education						
Less than high school	39.2%	35.9%	37.5%	37.1%	40.7%	24.8%
High school degree	37.1	39.3	38.3	38.9	35.7	40.5
Some college	23.7	24.8	24.2	24.0	23.7	34.8
Total	100.0%	100.0%	100.0%	100.0%	100.1%	100.1%
(N)	(194)	(326)	(347)	(455)	(241)	(1309)
Region						
South	51.5%	44.2%	44.4%	38.6%	46.1%	21.3%
Non-South	48.5	55.8	55.6	61.4	53.9	78.7
Total	100.0%	100.0%	100.0%	100.0%	100.0%	100.0%
(N)	(194)	(326)	(347)	(456)	(241)	(1311)
Race						
White	86.0%	90.5%	88.2%	90.1%	85.8%	91.9%
Non-South	14.0	9.5	11.8	9.9	14.2	8.1
Total	100.0%	100.0%	100.0%	100.0%	100.0%	100.0%
(N)	(193)	(325)	(346)	(455)	(240)	(1301)
Sex						
Male	41.2%	40.2%	40.1%	39.3%	41.1%	49.5%
Female	58.8	59.8	59.9	60.7	58.9	50.5
Total	100.0%	100.0%	100.0%	100.0%	100.0%	100.0%
(N)	(194)	(326)	(347)	(456)	(241)	(1310)

Table 8
SOCIAL COMPOSITION OF EVANGELICALS
ACCORDING TO TYPE OF EVANGELICALS
(Whites only)

Social Category	Christianity Today Poll 1978-79			
	Conv. Evan.	Conf. Evan.	"Parallel" Evan.	Non- Evan.
Age				
18-34	23.8%	24.1%	25.1%	39.1%
35-55	43.9	35.9	39.4	31.9
56+	32.3	40.0	35.5	29.0
Total	100.0%	100.0%	100.0%	100.0%
(N)	(164)	(290)	(203)	(1183)
				v=.15*
Education				
Less than high school degree	36.1%	33.7%	37.9%	24.1%
High school degree	38.0	39.8	36.9	41.0
Some college	25.9	26.5	25.2	34.9
Total	100.0%	100.0%	100.0%	100.0%
(N)	(166)	(294)	(206)	(1195)
				v=.09*
Sex				
Male	44.6%	42.2%	43.2%	48.7%
Female	55.4	57.8	56.8	51.3
Total	100.0%	100.0%	100.0%	100.0%
(N)	(166)	(294)	(206)	(1196)
				phi=.04
Region				
South	49.4%	43.2%	44.2%	21.8%
Non-South	50.6	56.8	55.8	78.2
Total	100.0%	100.0%	100.0%	100.0%
(N)	(166)	(294)	(206)	(1196)
				phi=.18*

*Chi-square statistically significant at .001 level

137

Table 9
COMPARISON OF SOCIAL COMPOSITION OF EVANGELICALS AND NON-EVANGELICALS ACCORDING TO DIFFERENT SURVEYS OVER TIME
(Whites only)

Social Category	CT 1978-79 Non-Evan.	Evan.	Mich. 1980 Non-Evan.	Evan.	Mich. 1984 Non-Evan.	Evan.
Percent of Total Sample	85.3%	14.7%	85.0%	15.0%	83.2%	16.8%
(N)	(1196)	(206)	(1039)	(183)	(1431)	(288)
Age						
18-34	39.1%	25.1%	38.5%	36.1%	37.5%	35.1%
35-55	31.9	39.4	31.8	30.1	34.4	31.6
56+	29.0	35.5	29.7	33.9	28.0	33.3
Total	100.0%	100.0%	100.0%	100.1%	99.9%	100.0%
(N)	(1183)	(203)	(1039)	(183)	(1420)	(288)
	v=.10**		v=.03		v=.04	
Education						
Less than high school	24.1%	37.9%	21.8%	29.5%	17.8%	26.6%
High school degree	41.0	36.9	36.1	38.3	35.8	39.9
Some college	34.9	25.2	42.1	32.3	46.3	33.6
Total	100.0%	100.0%	100.0%	100.1%	99.9%	100.1%
(N)	(1195)	(206)	(1036)	(183)	(1424)	(286)
	v=.11**		v=.08*		v=.11**	
Region						
South	21.8%	44.2%	22.2%	44.8%	20.7%	44.8%
Non-South	78.2	55.8	77.8	55.2	79.3	55.2
Total	100.0%	100.0%	100.0%	100.0%	100.0%	100.0%
(N)	(1196)	(206)	(1039)	(183)	(1431)	(288)
	phi=.18**		phi=.18**		phi=.20**	
Sex						
Male	48.7%	43.2%	45.7%	33.3%	46.8%	34.7%
Female	51.3	56.8	54.3	66.7	53.2	65.3
Total	100.0%	100.0%	100.0%	100.0%	100.0%	100.0%
(N)	(1196)	(206)	(1039)	(183)	(1431)	(288)
	phi=.04		phi=.09*		phi=.09**	

*Chi-square statistically significant at .01 level
**Chi-square statistically significant at .001 level

Table 10
COMPARISON OF SOCIAL COMPOSITION OF EVANGELICALS AND NON-EVANGELICALS IN VARIOUS SURVEYS OVER TIME
(White Protestants and Catholics only)

Social Category	Anti-Sem. 1964		Unch. Amer. 1978		Anti-Sem. 1981		CT 1978-79		Conn. Mut. 1980		Mich. 1980		Mich. 1984	
	Non-Evan.	Evan.	Non-Evan.	Evan.	Non-Evan.	Evan.	Non-Evan.	Evan.	Non-Evan.	Evan.	Non-Evan.	Evan.	Non-Evan.	Evan.
Percent of Total Sample	80.1%	19.9%	69.2%	30.8%	81.4%	18.6%	87.5%	12.5%	70.8%	29.2%	82.5%	17.5%	78.2%	21.8%
Age:														
18-34	33.5%	33.2%	41.1%	28.6%	41.8%	33.3%	34.2%	22.0%	40.5%	29.4%	36.1%	34.4%	37.7%	30.9%
35-55	40.0	38.2	32.2	32.6	29.0	32.6	34.5	39.6	47.2	50.5	33.3	29.5	31.2	37.1
56+*	26.5	28.7	26.7	38.8	29.1	34.1	31.3	38.4	12.2	20.2	30.6	36.1	31.1	32.0
Education:														
Less than high school	44.9%	45.6%	29.0%	31.3%	18.9%	25.2%	27.6%	32.7%	27.8%	36.6%	23.9%	29.3%	21.9%	24.1%
High school degree	31.1	36.4	36.6	36.3	36.4	35.9	42.9	38.4	38.0	37.9	36.7	37.3	37.2	37.2
College	24.0	17.9	34.3	32.4	44.7	38.9	29.5	28.9	34.2	25.4	39.4	33.5	41.0	38.7
Region:														
South	20.0%	42.7%	22.4%	33.7%	**	**	24.0%	49.7%	**	**	28.2%	49.7%	22.9%	39.5%
Non-South	80.0	57.3	77.6	66.3	**	**	76.0	50.3	**	**	71.8	50.3	77.1	60.5
Sex:														
Male	42.8%	41.2%	52.1%	40.6%	49.8%	40.9%	42.7%	43.4%	50.7%	35.9%	44.0%	33.0%	44.7%	35.3%
Female	57.2	58.8	47.9	59.4	50.2	59.1	57.3	56.6	49.3	64.1	56.0	67.0	55.3	64.7

*Connecticut Mutual categories for age are 35-64 and 65-and-above
**No data available

Table 11
PERCENTAGE OF EVANGELICALS
WITHIN DIFFERENT EDUCATION LEVELS
CONTROLLING FOR THE AGE OF THE RESPONDENT
(Michigan study, 1984, White only)

Age	Less than high school degree	High school degree	Some college
17-34 Years			
Non-Evangelical	78.9%	83.9%	85.0%
Evangelical	21.1	16.1	15.0
Total	100.0%	100.0%	100.0%
(N)	(57)	(249)	(326)
		v=.05	
		sign=.519	
35-55 Years			
Non-Evangelical	78.8%	80.0%	89.0%
Evangelical	21.3	20.0	11.0
Total	100.1%	100.0%	100.0%
(N)	(80)	(210)	(290)
		v=.13	
		sign=.008	
56+			
Non-Evangelical	75.5%	80.2%	88.7%
Evangelical	24.5	19.8	11.3
Total	100.0%	100.0%	100.0%
(N)	(192)	(162)	(133)
		v=.13	
		sign=.012	

Table 12
RELIGIOUS CHARACTERISTICS OF EVANGELICALS
AND NON-EVANGELICALS (Whites only)

Religious Characteristic	Mich. 1980 Non-Evan.	Mich. 1980 Evan.	Mich. 1984 Non-Evan.	Mich. 1984 Evan.
Church Attendance				
Weekly or more	23.4%	50.3%	22.3%	46.5%
One to three times per month	23.7	23.5	24.6	27.8
Less than once per month	52.9	26.2	53.2	25.7
Total	100.0%	100.0%	100.1%	100.0%
(N)	(916)	(183)	(1283)	(288)
Religion Provides Guidance in Day-to-Day Living (asked only of those respondents who said religion was an important part of their life).				
A great deal	38.3%	69.9%	37.4%	70.1%
Quite a bit	29.1	21.3	32.3	18.3
Some	32.6	8.7	30.4	11.5
Total	100.0%	99.9%	100.1%	99.9%
(N)	(700)	(183)	(995)	(288)

Table 13
RELIGIOUS CHARACTERISTICS OF EVANGELICALS
ACCORDING TO TYPE OF EVANGELICAL (Whites only)

Religious Characteristic	Evangelical Voter, 1983 Conv. Evan.	Evangelical Voter, 1983 Conf. Evan.
Fundamentalist		
Yes	19.4%	21.4%
No	80.6	78.6
Total	100.0%	100.0%
(N)	(170)	(276)
Watch Religious Programs on TV		
Once a week or more	32.9%	26.8%
One to three times a month	14.1	13.4
Several times a year or less	52.9	59.8
Total	99.9%	100.0%
(N)	(170)	(276)
Evaluation of Religious TV Programs		
Favorable	59.4%	51.4%
Unsure	14.1	14.9
Unfavorable	26.4	33.7
Total	99.9%	100.0%
(N)	(170)	(276)

Table 14
RELIGIOUS PRACTICES OF EVANGELICALS
AND NON-EVANGELICALS
ACCORDING TO TYPE OF EVANGELICAL
(Whites only)

Religious Practices	*Christianity Today* Poll 1978-79			
	Conv. Evan.	Conf. Evan.	"Parallel" Evan.	Non- Evan.
Bible Reading				
Daily	48.2%	35.4%	43.8%	7.0%
One to three times a week	33.5	36.5	34.5	15.3
One to three times a month	9.1	9.4	8.9	11.6
Less than once a month	9.2	18.8	12.8	66.2
Total	100.0%	100.1%	100.0%	100.1%
(N)	(164)	(288)	(203)	(1097)
Church Attendance				
Weekly	75.8%	63.2%	68.8%	31.8%
One to three times a month	10.3	15.5	12.7	15.9
Less than once a month	13.9	21.3	18.5	52.2
Total	100.0%	100.0%	100.0%	99.9%
(N)	(165)	(291)	(205)	(1143)
Church Giving				
Ten percent or more	61.3%	47.9%	56.3%	10.8%
Five to nine percent	14.7	18.0	14.8	15.2
Less than five percent	24.0	34.1	28.9	73.9
Total	100.0%	100.0%	100.0%	99.9%
(N)	(150)	(261)	(183)	(1053)
Charismatic				
Yes	38.8%	29.2%	34.2%	16.5%
No	61.2	70.8	65.8	83.5
Total	100.0%	100.0%	100.0%	100.0%
(N)	(160)	(281)	(199)	(1108)
Speak in Tongues				
Yes	16.9%	10.3%	15.1%	01.0%
No	83.1	89.7	84.9	99.0
Total	100.0%	100.0%	100.0%	100.0%

142

Table 15
RELIGIOUS PRACTICES OF EVANGELICALS AND NON-EVANGELICALS IN VARIOUS SURVEYS OVER TIME (White Protestants and Catholics only)

Religious Practices	Anti-Sem. 1964		Unch. Amer. 1978		Anti-Sem. 1981		CT 1978-79		Mich. 1980		Mich. 1984	
	Non-Evan.	Evan.	Non-Evan.	Evan.	Non-Evan.	Evan.	Non-Evan.	Evan.	Non-Evan.	Evan.	Non-Evan.	Evan.
Church Attendance:												
Weekly/almost	61.6%	72.5%	38.0%	71.1%	36.5%	76.2%	40.6%	76.4%	35.9%	69.8%	32.6%	66.1%
1 or 2 times a month or less	38.4	27.5	62.0	28.9	63.5	23.8	59.4	23.6	64.1	30.2	67.4	33.9
Bible Reading:												
At least daily							10.7%	44.0%				
At least weekly							18.5	38.2				
Less than weekly/not at all							70.8	17.8				
Prayer:												
More than once a day			15.6%	45.9%								
Once a day			34.7	35.3								
Less often/never			49.7	18.8								
Church Member:												
Yes			55.2%	84.9%			75.3%	89.2%				
No			44.8	15.1			24.7	10.8				
Watch Religious Programs on TV:												
Yes			29.6%	55.3%			29.9%	52.9%				
No			70.4	44.7			70.1	47.1				
Tithe:												
Yes							14.9%	62.5%				
No							85.1	37.5				

Table 16
RELIGIOUS PRACTICES OF EVANGELICALS AND NON-EVANGELICALS
IN THE 1980 CONNECTICUT MUTUAL STUDY
(White Protestants and Catholics only)

Religious Practices	Frequently		Occasionally		Never	
	Non-Evan.	Evan.	Non-Evan.	Evan.	Non-Evan.	Evan.
Attend church services	33.3%	73.3%	44.7%	23.7%	21.8%	3.0%
Engage in prayer	47.8	86.9	39.0	13.1	13.2	0
Listen to religious broadcasts	11.6	36.3	37.9	48.3	50.5	15.4
Read the Bible	14.3	57.5	52.2	38.2	33.5	4.4
Encourage others to turn to religion	12.2	49.6	30.8	40.7	57.0	9.7
Participate in a church social activity	14.4	46.6	37.0	40.1	48.6	13.3

Table 17
SUB-GROUP DIFFERENCES WITHIN EVANGELICALISM: THE *CHRISTIANITY TODAY* SURVEY
(White Protestants and Catholics only)

Control Variables	N=49 Confessional	N=20 Born Again	N=50 Pure Fundamentalist	N=10 Pure Charismatic	N=30 Born Again/ Fund./Char.	N=915 Non-Evangelical
Age:						
35	12.2%	30.0%	22.0%	10.0%	36.7%	34.2%
>55	51.0	30.0	32.0	60.0	26.7	31.3
Education: 12 years	34.7	35.0	32.0	40.0	26.6	27.6
Sex: Male	38.8	50.0	50.0	40.0	36.7	42.7
Region: South	46.9	55.0	44.0	60.0	56.7	24.0
Read Bible daily	21.3	40.0	54.0	50.0	63.3	10.7
Attend Church weekly	63.8	80.0	82.0	70.0	86.7	40.6
Tithe	40.9	53.3	75.0	44.4	85.7	14.9
Church volunteer work	65.3	85.0	80.0	80.0	80.0	42.2
Share religious views with others monthly or more	57.8	70.6	77.8	60.0	66.7	33.3
Church member	87.5	90.0	94.0	90.0	83.3	75.3
Knows Bible verse	65.9	86.7	77.8	75.0	86.7	47.8
Abortion unacceptable	31.3	21.1	30.0	40.0	30.0	21.3
Homosexuality wrong	90.0	100.0	95.7	100.0	93.1	74.7
Respondent drinks alcohol	37.5	45.0	20.0	40.0	23.3	68.1
No obligation to help solve poverty problems	10.6	10.0	6.4	0	0	17.7
Party Identification:						
Republican	37.0	25.0	33.3	40.0	20.0	24.6
Independent	25.0	21.7	27.1	10.0	46.7	30.8
Democratic	50.0	41.3	39.6	50.0	33.3	44.6

Table 18
LIFE SATISFACTIONS: 1980 CONNECTICUT MUTUAL SURVEY
MEAN SCORES
(Protestants and Catholics only)

Life Satisfaction Variables	Evangelicals		Non-Evangelicals	
	Protestants	Catholics	Protestants	Catholics
Happy with leisure time	1.46*	1.54	1.62	1.60
Happy with work	1.41	1.46	1.66	1.59
Happy with friends	1.29	1.49	1.41	1.46
Happy with spouse	1.22	1.29	1.33	1.46
Happy with family, relatives	1.22	1.31	1.34	1.38
Happy with religion	1.25	1.51	1.78	1.76
Happy with life as a whole	1.35	1.32	1.57	1.59
Totals	265	43	521	319

*1=very happy
2=happy
3=unhappy
4=very unhappy

Table 19
THE ISSUE ORIENTATIONS OF EVANGELICALS AND
NON-EVANGELICALS OVER TIME
(Whites only)

Issue Scale	1980		1984	
	Non-Evan.	Evan.	Non-Evan.	Evan.
Ideology	4.37	4.92*	4.47	5.35*
	(755)	(119)	(1236)	(254)
Reduce Government Services	3.82	3.89	4.13	4.18
	(862)	(152)	(1283)	(168)
Government Aid to Minorities	5.20	5.84*	4.17	4.62*
	(1039)	(183)	(1256)	(251)
Government Guarantee of Jobs	4.57	4.55	4.34	4.40
	(878)	(148)	(1249)	(244)
Defense Spending	5.24	5.44	3.93	4.41*
	(906)	(167)	(1283)	(258)
Cooperation with Soviet Union	2.77	3.68*	4.02	4.69*
	(974)	(171)	(1252)	(240)
Role of Women	2.77	3.68*	2.67	3.61*
	(974)	(171)	(1304)	(264)
Prayer in Public Schools	3.70	4.60*	3.52	4.53*
	(862)	(177)	(1104)	(266)
Abortion	2.23	2.91*	2.02	2.83*
	(1009)	(177)	(1389)	(281)

NOTE: Decimal figures are mean scores on the indicated issue scale. A higher score indicates a more conservative orientation.
*F significant at .001 level

Table 20
POLICY PREFERENCES AND
OTHER POLITICAL ATTITUDES OF EVANGELICALS:
THE EVANGELICAL VOTER SURVEY
(White Protestants and Catholics only)

Policy Positions	Evangelicals N=592
Favor nuclear freeze	40.1 %
Oppose nuclear freeze	37.7
Favor ERA	47.0
Oppose ERA	31.3
Favor increase defense spending	42.7
Oppose increase defense spending	30.2
Favor birth control information in the schools	64.2
Oppose birth control information in the schools	27.5
Agree abortion should not be legal for any reason	28.4
Disagree abortion should not be legal for any reason	66.5
Agree abortion should be legally available for any woman who desires	34.4
Disagree abortion should be legally available for any woman who desires	59.5
Agree that government should provide abortion aid for poor women	25.0
Disagree that government should provide abortion aid for poor women	66.2
Agree AIDS is God's punishment for homosexual lifestyle	34.3
Disagree AIDS is God's punishment for homosexual lifestyle	47.9
Know and favor Jerry Falwell	28.0
Don't know/no opinion of Jerry Falwell	43.6
Know and oppose Jerry Falwell	28.4
Dislike Roman Catholic Church	24.8
Neutral toward Roman Catholic Church	22.5
Like Roman Catholic Church	52.7

Table 21
PARTISAN SELF-IMAGES AMONG EVANGELICALS
AND NON-EVANGELICALS ACCORDING TO
TYPE OF EVANGELICAL (Whites only)

Partisan Self-Image	Conv. Evan.	Conf. Evan.	"Parallel" Evan.	Non- Evan.
	Christianity Today Poll 1978-79			
Democrat	41.9%	38.6%	42.5%	43.7%
Independent	28.8	28.1	29.0	34.1
Republican	29.4	33.3	28.5	22.3
Total	100.1%	100.0%	100.0%	100.1%
(N)	(160)	(285)	(200)	(1145)

Table 22
PARTISANSHIP AND IDEOLOGY OF EVANGELICALS AND NON-EVANGELICALS IN VARIOUS SURVEYS OVER TIME
(White Protestants and Catholics only)

Political Characteristic	Anti-Sem. 1984 Non-Evan.	Anti-Sem. 1984 Evan.	CT 1979 Non-Evan.	CT 1979 Evan.	Conn. Mut. 1980 Non-Evan.	Conn. Mut. 1980 Evan.	Mich. 1980 Non-Evan.	Mich. 1980 Evan.	Anti-Sem. 1981 Non-Evan.	Anti-Sem. 1981 Evan.	Mich. 1984 Non-Evan.	Mich. 1984 Evan.
Partisanship:												
Democratic	45.7%	51.1%	44.5%	41.4%	35.5%	42.3%	35.1%	39.7%	39.8%	30.4%	34.9%	31.1%
Independent	23.0	18.9	30.9	27.7	36.1	26.8	37.1	30.4	28.9	32.1	33.5	32.7
Republican	31.3	30.0	24.6	30.9	28.5	30.8	27.9	29.9	31.3	37.5	31.7	36.2
Ideology:												
Liberal	*	*	*	*	22.1%	12.4%	8.7%	3.4%	18.2%	8.4%	10.2%	8.9%
Moderate	*	*	*	*	50.2	47.5	69.4	53.8	40.1	32.8	70.6	53.6
Conservative	*	*	*	*	27.7	40.1	21.8	42.7	41.8	58.8	19.2	37.5

*No data available
The Unchurched American Study had no partisanship or ideology variables.

Table 23
POLITICAL ORIENTATIONS OF EVANGELICALS
AND NON-EVANGELICALS OVER TIME
(Whites only)

Political Orientations	Mich. 1980		Mich. 1984	
	Non-Evan.	Evan.	Non-Evan.	Evan.
Partisan Affection				
Polarized Democrat	14.9%	7.9%	21.1%	12.7%
Simple Democrat	12.8	15.9	10.2	7.2
Amplified Democrat	13.8	17.2	6.8	8.5
Neutral	21.4	15.2	7.6	5.9
Amplified Republican	11.7	17.2	13.4	13.1
Simple Republican	11.0	11.9	14.2	19.9
Polarized Republican	14.5	14.6	26.7	32.6
Total	100.1%	99.9%	100.0%	99.9%
(N)	(779)	(151)	(1146)	(236)

Table 24
POLITICAL CHARACTERISTICS OF EVANGELICALS
ACCORDING TO TYPE OF EVANGELICAL
(Whites only)

Political Characteristic	Evangelical Voter 1983	
	Conv. Evan.	Conf. Evan.
Ideology		
Conservative	72.9%	67.0%
Moderate	7.6	9.4
Liberal	19.4	23.6
Total	99.9%	100.0%
(N)	(170)	(276)
Moral Majority		
Know/Favorable	38.2%	32.2%
Never Heard/Don't Know	34.1	37.7
Know/Unfavorable	27.6	30.1
Total	99.9%	100.0%
(N)	(170)	(276)

Table 25
SELECTED POLITICAL ATTITUDES OF EVANGELICALS
AND NON-EVANGELICALS OVER TIME
(Whites only)

Political Attitude	Mich. 1980		Mich. 1984	
	Non-Evan.	Evan.	Non-Evan.	Evan.
Which one of the following goals seems *most* desirable to you?				
Maintaining order in nation	23.3%	28.9%	30.3%	27.0%
Giving people more say in important political decisions	12.9	17.2	25.3	29.1
Fighting rising prices	46.2	40.6	23.0	24.1
Protecting freedom of speech	17.6	13.3	21.4	19.9
Total	100.0%	100.0%	100.0%	100.0%
(N)	(1016)	(180)	(687)	(141)
Rating of "Evangelical groups active in politics, such as the Moral Majority" (thermometer scale from 0 degrees indicating cold, negative feelings, to 50 degrees indicating neutral to 100 degrees indicating warm, positive feelings)				
65-100 degrees	14.4%	42.9%	14.9%	39.2%
51-64 degrees	11.3	12.3	11.7	17.5
50 degrees	28.1	24.4	26.2	25.1
35-49 degrees	11.7	11.0	14.2	8.4
0-34 degrees	34.5	12.3	33.0	9.9
Total	100.0%	99.9%	100.0%	100.1%
(N)	(917)	(154)	(1271)	(263)

Table 26
CORRELATIONS WITH THE FALWELL PLATFORM

Social Demographic Variables		Religious Variables		Social/Political Attitudes	
Age	.18[a]	Fundamentalist Denomination	.21	Moral Majority	.13
Education	−.12			Jerry Falwell	.31
Income	−.10	Born Again	.23	Billy Graham	.09
Socio-economic Status	−.13[b]	Fundamentalist Self-Identification	.22	*Sword of the Lord*[h]	.07
Region	−.08[c]	Biblical Literalism	.13	Dislike Roman Catholic Church	.24
Sex/Employment	−.08[d]	Born Again/ Fundamentalist/ Literalist	.33	Conservatism	.30

[a] Correlations are Pearson product moment correlations.

[b] Combines education and Income

[c] 1=South 2=Non-South

[d] 1=Male 2=Female at home 3=Female employed

Religiosity[e]	.39
Salience of religion for politics[f]	.43
Pastoral political activism[g]	.02

Support for Republican party[i]	.15
Conservative/ Republican	.26

[h] Fundamentalist publication

[i] Support for the Republican party is a composite of Republican party registration and usual Republican voting habits

[e] A measure of religious involvement including church attendance, importance of religion to respondent, and religious television viewing

[f] A measure of the importance of religion in politics for the respondent

[g] A measure of pastoral involvement including sermons, and other statements of political positions

Table 27
PREDICTING THE FALL PLATFORM:
BEST FIT REGRESSIONS

Social Demographic Variables		Beta	Sig.
Age		.10	.01
Sex/employment		−.08	.04
Religious Variables			
Fundamentalist denominational		.09	.02
Born again/fundamentalist/biblical literalist*		.10	.02
Religiosity/religious political salience**		.27	.001
Social/Political Attitudes			
Jerry Falwell		.12	.002
Dislike Roman Catholic Church		.13	.001
Conservative/Republict		.22	.001
	Constant	.001	
	Multiple R	.57	
	R. Square	.32	

*An index combining three variables from the preceding table. At one end of the scale would be a person who is born again, identifies as a fundamentalist, and holds a literal view of Scripture. At the other end of the scale would be a respondent who answered in opposite fashion.

**Combines the religiosity and religious political salience variables from the preceding table into one index.

†Combines conservative political ideology and support for Republican party into one index.

Table 28
POLITICAL ATTITUDES ON CHURCH-STATE RELATIONS
ACCORDING TO TYPE OF EVANGELICAL
(Whites only)

Church-State Relations	Christianity Today Poll 1978-79			
	Conv. Evan.	Conf. Evan.	"Parallel" Evan.	Non- Evan.
Importance for religious organizations to make public statements about what they feel to be the will of God:				
Ethical-Moral Issues				
Very important	76.5%	64.3%	72.0%	32.0%
Fairly important	17.9	24.1	20.5	37.2
Not very important	5.6	11.5	7.5	30.8
Total	100.0%	99.9%	100.0%	100.0%
(N)	(162)	(286)	(200)	(1113)
Political-Economic Matters				
Very important	38.9%	31.0%	35.1%	16.8%
Fairly important	27.4	25.9	28.4	24.7
Not very important	33.8	43.1	36.6	58.5
Total	100.1%	100.0%	100.1%	100.0%
(N)	(157)	(274)	(194)	(1108)
Should religious organizations try to persuade senators and representatives to enact legislation they would like to see become law?				
Should	70.1	64.1	66.1	42.4
Should not	29.9	35.9	33.9	57.8
Total	100.0%	100.0%	100.0%	100.0%
(N)	(144)	(259)	(177)	(1030)

Table 29
ATTITUDES ON ROLE OF RELIGION IN POLITICS
ACCORDING TO TYPE OF EVANGELICAL
(Whites only)

Role of Religion	Evangelical Voter 1983	
	Conv. Evan.	Conf. Evan.
Should religious leaders and groups take a very active role in politics?		
No involvement	27.6%	35.1%
Unsure	11.2	11.6
Active role	61.2	53.3
Total	100.0%	100.0%
(N)	(170)	(276)
How important are the religious and moral views of a candidate for office in your voting decision?		
More important than almost any factor	22.3%	20.4%
About the same importance as other factors	59.6	57.6
Less important than most factors I take into account	18.1	21.9
Total	100.0%	99.9%
(N)	(166)	(269)

Table 30
ATTITUDES ON SOCIAL RESPONSIBILITY
ACCORDING TO TYPE OF EVANGELICAL
(Whites only)

Social Responsibility	*Christianity Today* Poll 1978-79			
	Conv. Evan.	Conf. Evan.	"Parallel" Evan.	Non- Evan.
Do you think that society as a whole has an obligation to see that children, the handicapped, and the elderly have their basic needs met or not?				
Yes	97.6%	98.3%	97.5%	97.2%
No	2.4	1.7	2.5	2.8
Total	100.0%	100.0%	100.0%	100.0%
(N)	(164)	(291)	(204)	(1161)
What do you think you should do about poverty in this community?				
Personally and directly help	24.7%	22.9%	25.1%	19.0%
Contribute to religious and community organizations	48.7	44.3	47.6	38.7
Persuade church, religious, and government organizations	18.8	21.0	19.4	19.7
Have no obligation beyond paying taxes	7.8	11.8	7.9	22.6
Total	100.0%	100.0%	100.0%	100.0%
(N)	(154)	(271)	(191)	(1041)
Which source should provide for societal needs?				
Government	17.4%	18.2%	18.7%	22.9%
Combination of government and voluntary organizations	71.8	72.0	71.1	69.8
Voluntary organizations and individuals	10.7	9.8	10.2	7.3
Total	99.9%	100.0%	100.0%	100.0%
(N)	(149)	(275)	(187)	(1097)

Table 31
POLITICAL PARTICIPATION OF EVANGELICALS
AND NON-EVANGELICALS
IN VARIOUS SURVEYS OVER TIME
(White Protestants and Catholics only)

Political	Anti-Sem. 1964		Anti-Sem. 1981		Mich. 1980		Mich. 1984	
	Non-Evan.	Evan.	Non-Evan.	Evan.	Non-Evan.	Evan.	Non-Evan.	Evan.
Vote Turnout:								
Yes	76.0%	69.3%	77.3%	76.7%	72.1%	77.3%	75.3%	75.4%
No	24.0	30.7	22.7	23.3	27.9	22.7	24.7	24.6
Campaign Sticker:								
Yes					8.0%	5.9%	8.6%	8.6%
No					92.0	94.1	91.4	91.4
Attend political meetings:								
Yes					7.9%	7.0%	8.4%	4.2%
No					92.1	93.0	91.6	95.8
Work for party/candidate:								
Yes					4.2%	3.8%	3.7%	2.1%
No					95.8	96.2	96.3	97.9
Give money to campaign:								
Yes							14.3%	9.0%
No							85.7	91.0

Table 32
POLITICAL PARTICIPATION OF EVANGELICALS
AND NON-EVANGELICALS OVER TIME
(Whites only)

Political Participation	Mich. 1980		Mich. 1984	
	Non-Evan.	Evan.	Non-Evan.	Evan.
Voted in presidential election				
Yes	71.5%	77.0%	76.2%	70.1%
No	28.5	23.0	23.8	29.9
Total	100.0%	100.0%	100.0%	100.0%
(N)	(1039)	(183)	(1431)	(288)
Tried to influence others				
Yes	30.3%	30.8%	34.2%	31.9%
No	69.7	69.2	65.8	68.1
Total	100.0%	100.0%	100.0%	100.0%
(N)	(1018)	(172)	(1384)	(288)
Attended rally, speech, dinner				
Yes	7.5%	6.4%	8.4%	3.5%
No	92.5	93.6	91.6	96.5
Total	100.0%	100.0%	100.0%	100.0%
(N)	(1018)	(172)	(1387)	(288)
Worked for a candidate				
Yes			4.5%	1.7%
No			95.5	98.3
Total			100.0%	100.0%
(N)			(1386)	(286)
Made political contribution				
Yes			14.4%	8.4%
No			85.6	91.6
Total			100.0%	100.0%
(N)			(1385)	(286)

Table 33
THE VOTING BEHAVIOR OF EVANGELICALS AND NON-EVANGELICALS OVER TIME
(Whites only)

	Mich. 1980		Mich. 1984	
	Non-Evan.	Evan.	Non-Evan.	Evan.
Recalled Vote in 1976				
Carter	47.5%	50.5%		
Ford	52.5	49.5		
Total	100.0%	100.0%		
(N)	(668)	(111)		
	phi=.02			
Reported Vote in 1980				
Anderson	10.8%	1.4%		
Carter	33.6	32.6		
Reagan	55.6	66.0		
Total	100.0%	100.0%		
(N)	(702)	(141)		
	v=.13**			
Reported Vote in 1980				
Carter	37.7%	33.1%		
Reagan	62.3	66.9		
Total	100.0%	100.0%		
(N)	(626)	(139)		
	phi=.04			
Reported Vote in 1984				
Mondale			39.0%	23.9%
Reagan			61.0	76.1
Total			100.0%	100.0%
(N)			(1023)	(197)
			phi=.12**	
Reported Vote for U.S. Representative				
Democrat	51.7%	43.3%	52.9%	45.3%
Republican	48.3	56.7	47.1	54.7
Total	100.0%	100.0%	100.0%	100.0%
(N)	(644)	(127)	(888)	(179)
	phi=.06		phi=.06	
Reported Vote for U.S. Senator				
Democrat	52.3%	39.3%	48.5%	46.1%
Republican	47.7	60.7	51.5	53.9
Total	100.0%	100.0%	100.0%	100.0%
(N)	(463)	(84)	(518)	(128)
	phi=.09*		phi=.02	

*Chi-square statistically significant at .05 level
**Chi-square statistically significant at .001 level

Table 34
VOTING PREFERENCES OF EVANGELICALS AND
NON-EVANGELICALS IN VARIOUS SURVEYS OVER TIME
(White Protestants and Catholics only)

Political	Anti-Sem. 1964		Anti-Sem. 1981		Mich. 1980		Mich. 1984	
	Non-Evan.	Evan.	Non-Evan.	Evan.	Non-Evan.	Evan.	Non-Evan.	Evan.
Recalled Vote in 1960:								
Kennedy	59.3%	47.4%						
Nixon	40.8	52.6						
Projected Vote in 1964:								
Johnson	62.1%	57.6%						
Goldwater	31.5	36.1						
Uncertain	6.4	6.3						
Recalled Vote in 1976:								
Carter					45.6%	50.9%		
Ford					54.4	49.1		
Reported Vote in 1980:								
Anderson			10.9%	5.1%	9.4%	2.1%		
Carter			31.6	28.6	33.6	33.8		
Reagan			57.6	66.3	57.0	64.1		
Reported Vote in 1980:								
Carter					37.1%	34.5%		
Reagan					62.9	65.5		
Reported Vote in 1984:								
Mondale							35.5%	28.2%
Reagan							64.5	71.8

Appendices

Appendix A

To a great degree, the measurement of the concept of evangelical has been left to the Gallup organization and has been left pretty much untouched by scholars. Gallup defines evangelicals as those who have the following three basic characteristics: "They describe themselves as 'born-again Christians' or they say they have had a 'born-again' experience; they have encouraged other people to believe in Jesus Christ; and they believe in a literal interpretation of the Bible." Gallup has measured evangelicalism by two experiential variables: having been born again and having witnessed. One doctrinal question is included, attitudes toward the Scriptures. Gallup says that the latter "is a fairly strict definition, because some evangelicals do not hold to a literal interpretation of the Bible, although they accept the absolute authority of the Bible."

We ran a test with the data from the Gallup "Unchurched American" study to see if those who hold the "inspired" opinion belong in the evangelical category. We place with the "literal" or "inerrant" group those who believe that Jesus is either God or the Son of God and who believe in the resurrection of Jesus, have made a commitment to Christ, and believe in life after death; 314 respondents met these criteria.

In Table A we compare this new group of literal/inspired respondents with the original Gallup categorization and a third grouping which combined all respondents who had given either a literal or an inspired response into one category. We label these three categorizations as follows: (1) literal (the original Gallup category), (2) inspired (but orthodox), and (3) inspired (but not orthodox). We compare these groups on a set of questions that should differentiate serious believers from those who take their religion less seriously.

Table A
COMPARISON OF GALLUP CATEGORY OF BIBLICAL LITERALISTS
WITH A GROUP OF BIBLICAL INSPIRATIONALISTS
WHO HOLD OTHER ORTHODOX BELIEFS:
UNCHURCHED AMERICAN SURVEY
(All respondents included)

	Literal (N=675)	Inspired but Orthodox (N=314)	Inspired/ Not Orthodox (N=500)
Religion very important in life	70.9%	70.2%	31.4%
Had religious training as adult	16.5%	20.3%	9.4%
Have had a "religious" experience	46.5%	45.9%	16.9%
Ever gone two years or more without church	34.0%	33.3%	44.4%
Pray constantly/prayer is my life	18.4%	17.3%	4.0%
Born again plus witness	20.1%	19.8%	3.0%

Orthodox = Belief in Jesus as God or Son of God
  Belief in the resurrection
  Made a commitment to Jesus
  Belief in life after death

Note that the newly created "inspired but orthodox" category is very similar to the original Gallup literal category and substantially different from the "Bible is inspired but not orthodox" category. Clearly, a person who believes that the Bible is the inspired word of God, shares what we have called evangelical doctrine, and has made a commitment to Christ should not be excluded from evangelical membership.

In summary, the Gallup measures place too great an emphasis on experience and too little emphasis on doctrine. In addition, the one doctrinal question on attitudes toward the Bible fails to include as evangelicals those who feel that the Bible is the inspired word of God and hold doctrinal positions consistent with traditional orthodoxy. We have also argued that the born-again language is likely to turn off individuals from a confessional tradition. Finally we feel that witnessing is not an essential characteristic of an evangelical while arguing that the Gallup item needs clarification regarding frequency and type.

Appendix B

HOW TO STUDY EVANGELICALISM
BY SECONDARY ANALYSIS

In working with these data files, our initial task was to identify the number of evangelicals in each study. The task was difficult because no two studies used the same set of measures. For subsequent studies we advocate the following procedures:

1. Identify evangelicals from the potential measures of evangelicalism in each of the particular survey instruments. In some of the studies we considered, several measures were present; more often there were only a few. This forced us into thinking through questions such as what the minimal criteria are for identifying a person as a potential evangelical. We feel that evangelical Christianity is first and foremost Christ-centered Christianity. And, in particular, the focus should be on the role of Christ in providing salvation for the sins of mankind through his birth, life, death, resurrection, and coming again. Many Christian traditions make this conception central to their theology, but it is the sine qua non for an evangelical. If survey instruments do not have measures to tap this dimension, they are not useful in identifying evangelicals.

Is being Christ-centered identical with being born again? We think not. Making born-again status a defining characteristic of an evangelical is a mistake if christological measures are available. Not all evangelicals will have had a born-again experience. Accepting Christ as Savior and Lord can occur by means other than a born-again experience. One may have accepted Christ for as long as one can remember, having been raised in the faith. In addition, one may associate a born-again experience with a sudden Saul/Paul type of conversion experience, and this may seem foreign to the believer. Hence born-again status is not the critical defining characteristic of an evangelical; it is his or her beliefs about Christ. The born-again experience is *how* one came to faith, not a defining characteristic of the faith. For the person comfortable with the born-again language and who understands it in the deeper sense that Christ intended when he instructed Nicodemus that "Ye must be born again," then the relationship between saying that one has had the experience and appropriate christology should be strong. In other words, a born-again believer can be expected to accept the appropriate christological measures, whatever they may be, in the survey.

For our purposes, then, a born-again item is tertiary in identifying evangelicals. It should always be used as a supplement to items concerning Christ's birth, life, death, and resurrection and, in particular, with Christ's central role in salvation. If no christological items are present but a born-again item is, the latter should be used with extreme caution, since there is some evidence of unreliability when the item is used as a key measure of evangelicalism. On the other hand, the born-again item can be helpful in distinguishing between orthodox or confessional evangelicals who are uncomfortable with the concept and other evangelicals who are. For example, Lutherans are much less likely to claim born-again status than are Baptists. This is the case in every study we have examined.

Assuming some christological measures in a survey, how do we know that they are measuring evangelical faith in a valid manner? Respondents who give the appropriate christological responses can be weeded out by their answers to other questions. Two examples from extant studies will illustrate the point. First, in the study conducted by the Connecticut Mutual Life Insurance Company, respondents who claimed to have made a commitment to Christ were asked to rank the importance of salvation and also whether they had ever had "something you call a religious experience." Failure to rank salvation as very important and claiming "never" to have had a religious experience ruled a person out of the evangelical category. Second, in the *Christianity Today* survey conducted by Gallup, respondents were judged not to be evangelicals if they said that the Devil does not exist, that the origin of man is unknown, and that salvation is not important.

Is the christological criterion enough? We think not. Four other aspects seem indispensable to evangelical faith: (a) recognizing the Bible as a guide to faith and life; (b) seeing God not as an impersonal force in the world but as actively involved, as infinite yet personal; (c) seeing mankind as sinful and in need of God's saving grace; and (d) putting a central emphasis on spreading the Good News, evangelism and missions.

The survey instruments we examined were deficient with respect to these criteria, all of which are important for valid evangelical classification. Ideally, each dimension should be measured with multiple items. This is what we would term a maximal measurement strategy. To be considered an evangelical, an individual would have to be Christ-centered; believe in an authoritative Bible inspired by God; see God as active, infinite yet personal; see mankind as sinful; and accept the centrality of evangelism and mission. Under the minimal measurement strategy, on the other hand, the individual would simply have to respond positively to christological measures to be classified an evangelical. Obviously, there are likely to be more evangelicals under the minimal strategy. It is easier to meet condition A than conditions A through

E. And yet under condition A, errors in assignment are quite possible, while under conditions A through E, errors are much more unlikely.

2. Identify a series of "pre-doctrinal" questions, items that say something important about the respondents that allow us to classify them as either non-evangelical or evangelical. Ideally, we were hoping to find items that asked respondents about their belief in God and their belief in life after death. Many individuals who are not evangelicals accept these pre-doctrinal criteria. Our argument, however, is that *all* evangelicals would attest to a belief in God and a belief in life after death.

To illustrate, from the *Christianity Today* study, three respondents who gave the evangelical response on the Bible (i.e., that it is God's word with no mistakes) said they did not believe in God, while twenty others said there is no life after death. From the same study, five who claimed Christ was God did not believe in God, while fully 67 others did not believe in life after death. Without some effort to rule out respondents based on their "pre-doctrinal" answers, errors in assignment to evangelical categories will occur.

3. Identify those who have no religious preference instead of relying on such more common identifications as "Protestant" or "Catholic." In almost every case a respondent who claims no religious preference will not meet other evangelical criteria. Individuals who give no religious preference when asked should have to "prove" on other questions that they meet evangelical criteria. If in doubt, researchers should exclude them from evangelical membership. Again, focusing on the *Christianity Today* survey, we found that 17 respondents with an inerrant view of Scripture said they had no religious preference, while an even larger number (52) accepted Christ as God and yet claimed no religious preference.

4. Identify respondents for whom religion appears to have little or no salience. Most of the studies we examined have measures of this kind: "Do you consider yourself a religious person?" (Connecticut Mutual); "Do you consider religion to be an important part of your life or not?" (Michigan, 1984); "All in all, how important would you say that religion is to you: extremely important, quite important, fairly important, not too important, not important at all?" (Glock/Stark, Anti-Semitism); "How much consolation and help would you say you get from your beliefs about God: a lot, fair amount, very little or not at all?" (*Christianity Today*). Our argument here is that people who say "no" to the first two questions, "not important" to the third, and "very little" or "not at all" to the last are candidates for exclusion from evangelical membership. Again, these respondents should have to "prove" their credentials elsewhere to be included.

We are suggesting the possibility of exclusion from evangelical status of those respondents who claim to attach little or no import to their religion. Is this justifiable? We think so unless there is overwhelming evidence to the contrary from other items measuring evangelicalism. Evidence suggests that respondents who attach low salience to their religion but score high on evangelical doctrinal items behave differently than those who give high salience to their religion and give appropriate evangelical responses on other items. (See Table B.) In fact, they give less "religious" answers on other questions, suggesting that their low salience responses should govern assignment into non-evangelical status (or at least into a "near evangelical" low salience category). For purposes of studying socio-political attitudes and behaviors, it is the high salience group that is most important. This group can be reached with messages about appropriate attitudes and behavior, while their low salience co-religionists may not even receive the cues.

Note that as the consolation and help that one receives from religion increases, doctrinal answers become more consistent with evangelical belief, and religiosity increases as well.

5. Identify individuals from denominations that are not Christ-centered (Jehovah's Witnesses, Mormons, Christian Scientists, Unitarians, etc.) and exclude them from the analysis. Failure to do this is a problem in study after study and inflates the number of evangelicals reported. We were unable to make such exclusions in this study because a number of the surveys did not provide enough detailed denominational information. The number of "misassigned" evangelicals does not exceed one percent in any of the studies where full denominational data are available; nonetheless, some misassignment occurs in every survey even where such data are present.

Table B
SALIENCE OF RELIGION AND
RELIGIOUS DOCTRINE AND BEHAVIOR:
CHRISTIANITY TODAY SAMPLE

Percentages that believe:	Consolation from One's Religion		
	Little/no consolation	Fair consolation	A lot of consolation
Jesus is God/Son of God	78.4	92.7	96.5
Jesus is the only hope for heaven	25.8	44.1	64.6
The Bible contains no mistakes	20.6	33.2	60.4
Evangelism is important	17.5	28.2	51.0
Salvation is important	8.2	14.2	48.7
They are born again	3.1	9.8	36.7
Percentages that:			
Regularly witness*	19.6	25.7	
Regularly attend church**	11.3	24.3	58.1
Regularly read the Bible	5.2	14.2	49.9
Tithe†	3.1	8.1	26.7
Do volunteer church work	27.8	30.7	57.7
Are church members	59.8	65.6	85.3

*"Regular" witnessing is considered at least once per month
**Regular church attendance and Bible reading are at least once per week
†Tithing involves giving at least ten percent of income to the church and other religious organizations

166

Appendix C

The following operational definitions were employed in differentiating between "conversionalist" and "confessional" evangelicals.

The Evangelical Voter

Conversionalist evangelicals were those white, "conventional" Protestants who (1) stated that the creation story in Genesis is either literally true or a true account of how God created the world, and (2) called themselves "born again" Christians, by which they mean to say that they had a conversion experience related to Jesus Christ.

Confessional evangelicals were those white, "conventional" Protestants who (1) stated that a person has to accept Jesus Christ personally as his or her savior in order to have eternal salvation and be saved from hell, and (2) stated that the creation story in Genesis is either literally true or a true account of how God created the world.

Christianity Today

Conversionist evangelicals were white Protestants who stated (1) that Christ was both fully God and fully man or that Jesus Christ was a man but was divine, the Son of God; (2) that the Bible is the word of God and is not mistaken in its statements and teachings, and (3) that they had had a born-again experience that involved Jesus Christ and represented a conversion experience that was still important to them at the time of the interview.

Confessional evangelicals were white Protestants who stated (1) that Christ was both fully God and fully man or that Jesus Christ was a man, but was divine, the Son of God, (2) that the Bible is the word of God and is not mistaken in its statements and teachings, and (3) that the only hope for heaven is through personal faith in Jesus Christ.

Parallel evangelicals were white Protestants who stated (1) that they had had a born-again experience, (2) that the Bible is the word of God and is not mistaken in its statements and teachings, and (3) that their religious beliefs about God gave them either "a lot" or "a fair amount" of consolation.

The 1980 and 1984 Michigan Studies:

Evangelicals were white, "conventional" Protestants who stated (1) that they had had a born-again experience, (2) that "the Bible is God's Word and all it says is true," and (3) that religion was an important part of their life.

Participants

Mark Amstutz
Department of Political Science
Wheaton College

Wendell Collins
The Rutherford Institute

Michael Cromartie
Ethics and Public Policy Center

Dean C. Curry
Department of History and Political
Science   Messiah College

Edward Dobson
Liberty University

Os Guinness
Theologian and Author
Oxford, England

James D. Hunter
Department of Sociology
University of Virginia

James Jordan
Geneva Ministries

Lyman Kellstedt
Department of Political Science
Wheaton College

Tim LaHaye
American Coalition for Traditional
Values

George Marsden
The Divinity School
Duke University

Richard Mouw
Fuller Theological Seminary

Kenneth A. Myers
This World

Ronald Nash
Department of Philosophy and
Religion
Western Kentucky University

Richard John Neuhaus
The Rockford Institute
Center on Religion and Society

Mark A. Noll
Department of History
Wheaton College

Ronald J. Sider
Eastern Baptist Theological Seminary

James W. Skillen
Association for Public Justice

Corwin Smidt
Department of Political Science
Calvin College

Paul T. Stallsworth
The Rockford Institute
Center on Religion and Society

Nicholas Wolterstorff
Department of Philosophy
Calvin College